Books in
World History
A Guide for Teachers and Students

W. Warren Wagar

Books in

World

History

A Guide for Teachers and Students

Indiana
University
Press
BLOOMINGTON & LONDON

for Robert H. Ferrell

Library of Congress catalog card number: 73–75791
ISBN: 0–253–31220–5 cl.

contents

foreword

At a professional gathering not long ago, an eminent educator told his audience that most history teachers were beyond saving. Their intelligence quotients were incredibly low; they understood little or nothing of their subject; the only solution lay in providing them with fool-proof classroom materials packages so completely programmed that fools like themselves could teach their students without having to think about it.

I do not doubt that the eminent educator had a point. Not yet having arrived in the millennium, we must reckon with the existence of thousands of teachers—college teachers, as well as high school teachers—who cannot teach or cannot master their discipline or (why doubt it?) cannot do either. I surrender these thousands to the producers of materials packages without a struggle.

But there are other thousands to whom the eminent educator's baleful indictment does not apply. This book is for them, and for students of history in and out of school who still believe in the power of the written word. Since they are probably the only people who are reading these lines, let me say: it is for you. It is written in the conviction that the more you and I think about our discipline and the more we read its literature, the higher will be the quality of our teaching and our learning.

Obviously, world history poses problems that students of national history may not find so formidable. More than once during the writing of this book, I was tempted to turn in my contract and forget about the whole thing. How could anyone (except perhaps those few scholars who have actually written full-dress surveys of world history) presume to recommend and discuss titles in all fields of history, ancient and modern, Eastern and Western, political and social? How could a single slender book make a credible dent in the literature of world history? Should I not plan to spend the next thirty years compiling a bibliography in at least one hundred volumes?

But every time I found myself lamenting the shortness of time and space, and the vastness of world history, and the continent-wide gaps in my own training, I remembered what is asked of teachers. Our graduate schools equip very few of them to teach anything more than regional history—American, European, East Asian, or Latin American. Yet their principals and chairmen expect them to teach world history. If many high school and not a few college teachers can gather up the courage to teach the stuff, surely any High and Mighty Herr Doktor Professor should be able to find the courage to supply them and their students with a short, manageable guide to its literature.

Inevitably, such a guide can offer only a sampling of that literature. The present one makes no claim to completeness; it does not even claim to mention all the "absolutely indispensable" books in any field, whatever criteria you choose for "indispensability." I only hope that I have spotlighted some of the problems you will face in sorting out your knowledge and some of the books that would help you most in gaining greater familiarity with your subject matter. In selecting books, I have given preference to recent titles over older ones; to titles in print; to titles available in paperback editions. I have not attempted to suggest primary sources, which obviously include all the world's prose and poetry, as well as all works of art, music, and architecture. I have steered clear of most titles specifically intended as classroom "textbooks." I have limited myself to works written in, or translated into, English.

These are drastic limitations. But do not think of this book as anything more than a gateway. In the titles reviewed, there are often massive bibliographies of primary and scholarly material that will lead you more deeply into any field you wish to study. In history, as in any other scholarly discipline, one good book always leads to another.

I have some people to thank. First, Robert H. Ferrell, of Indiana University, who first suggested that I write this book. Anyone who has had the kind fortune to study with Bob Ferrell knows the depth of his dedication to scholarship and teaching, and his strong aversion to humbug in all its forms. I dedicate this book to him.

I am also grateful to Daniel Miller, my graduate research assistant at the State University of New York at Binghamton. Throughout, I have had the firm support of Bernard Perry and Miriam S. Farley, of Indiana University Press. John E. Wiltz and John M. Thompson, also of Indiana University, have been most helpful.

Finally, I extend thanks and greetings to all my former associates in the History Education Project of the American Historical Association. *Books in World History* by no means bears the imprimatur of the Project, but had I not accepted the invitation to join in their work during the 1969–70 academic year, this book would probably never have been written. Very special thanks go to William Pulliam of the University of Delaware, from whose H.E.P. report on the teaching of world history in American high schools I learned much.

BINGHAMTON, NEW YORK
DECEMBER, 1972

Books in
World History
A Guide for Teachers and Students

a note on bibliographical data

All bibliographical information is taken from the 1972 edition of *Books in Print*. Dates given in brackets [ ] indicate the first edition of a book in its original language, and the letters U.P. stand for University Press.

If no price is listed, the book is not currently in print in the United States. Since the prices, editions, and availability of books are subject to constant change, readers should consult the latest volumes of *Books in Print* and *Paperbound Books in Print* in any library reference room or book store for up-to-date information.

A bullet (●) denotes that the book in question is particularly suitable for reading by high school students.

| chapter one | # Studying and Teaching World History |

1. The End of History?

As we enter the 1970's, the outlook for history in the classroom and the lecture hall is not bright. Some educators would use stronger language. A distinguished American historian, Charles G. Sellers, warns his colleagues of "the impending doom of historical learning in the schools." In Great Britain, Mary Price reports that many teachers "see a real danger of history disappearing from the time-table as a subject in its own right." David F. Kellum in his recent book *The Social Studies* prescribes euthanasia:

> Clio's case is terminal. Rather than make the attempt to revitalize her, I would suggest that she has lived out her normal life. The time has come to bring Clio to as swift and merciful an end as possible in the classroom, draw the curtain, toll the bell, give her a burial that befits a queen, and be done with it.

Even in the colleges and universities, the postwar boom in historical studies has perhaps ended at last. Students increasingly find other disciplines more relevant to their needs.

The end of history? This is no longer an unthinkable

thought. History figured very little in school or university curricula before the middle of the nineteenth century. It may shrink
to its previous obscurity in the last quarter of our own. Even if
patriotic organizations prevail upon school boards to spare the
study of American history from total extinction, what mercy can
the teacher of world history expect?

The study of history deserves a better fate. History
gives us insight that no other discipline can hope to provide. But
teachers and professional historians bear much of the blame for
their predicament. The scholar has for too many years cared too
little about the problems of teachers and the ways in which history can best be learned. The teacher has for too many years
imagined that students of history, unlike students of literature or
mathematics, need to be force-fed with huge helpings of "facts,"
just as the French farmer fattens his geese for the tables of
gourmets. In world history, especially, many of our texts are
dull; most of our students are bored; and all of us who teach feel
overwhelmed by the immensity of our subject.

Drastic solutions spring to mind, and some are being
tried in schools and colleges right now. If world history is un-
popular and badly taught and too big, why not replace it with
something a little more practical? Why not world "cultures"?
World "area studies"? World "problems"? Can't the student and
teacher of history profit from the findings of scholars in the
"other" social sciences?

There has never been a time in the history of our discipline when so many have searched so desperately for help from
workers in other fields. This search could be a sign of returning
health, rather than worsening illness, but too often it involves the
virtual abandonment of the values of historical study. The world
history course becomes world anthropology, world geography, or
world politics. In the panic to achieve up-to-dateness, the history
teacher may commit disciplinary suicide.

All reports to the contrary notwithstanding, there is a difference between history and the social sciences. Both study the past. But the social sciences are patterned after the natural sciences: they look for uniformities and regularities in human affairs. They discover laws, they build models, they invent ideal types. The historian may find such abstractions stimulating and useful, but he trains his eye on something else: the unique historical circumstances that distinguish every actual event from every other. He studies what philosophers call the "existential," the thing that actually happened to real human beings in real times and places.

This does not keep him from generalizing. He talks about classes, cities, countries, civilizations; even about the human race. But his product is a study of the unique. He tells us how, in spite of all the mechanical tendencies in life, in spite of all that is roughly predictable, chance and choice still make the actual behavior of human beings more problematic than the behavior of the social scientist's ideal types. Although history should and does borrow freely from the concepts of the social sciences, it more closely resembles the work of the realistic novelist, who gets down to raw particulars and paints life as it is.

Taking the "history" out of the world history course is therefore no answer to our problems. We must not throw out the baby with the bath water. In fact there is no better way to begin coping with the vastness of world history than to do some hard thinking about the study of history itself: its strategies of problem-solving, its research techniques, and its relationship to the other disciplines. The next few pages suggest books about the nature of history.

Carr, Edward Hallett, **What Is History?** (New York: Knopf, 1962. $4.95; Vintage paperback, $1.95). Few books on the problem of the nature of historical study have attracted so much favorable notice as Carr's. The author is a leading British historian of Soviet Russia. In *What Is History?* he ably defends the thesis that history is a science very much like any other, working under similar limitations, with similar methods of inquiry. He prefers the "great forces" to the "great man" theory of historical causation, and finds in history a record of relentless change and cumulative progress. The only difficulty is that Carr nowhere really answers his own question: what is history?

• Commager, Henry Steele, **The Nature and the Study of History** (Columbus: Merrill, 1965). One of the best known American historians defines history, gives shrewd advice about how to read and write it, and investigates such perennial problems as moral judgment, causation, and laws in history. The last chapter, by two professional educators, illustrates how five of Commager's general propositions can be applied in the school classroom. This is a volume in the Merrill Social Science Seminar Series. The five other volumes in the series are also recommended, as brief but authoritative introductions to each of the social sciences.

Elton, G. R., **The Practice of History** (New York: Crowell, 1968. $5.50; Apollo paperback, $2.25). "A manifesto rather than a treatise"—so Elton describes his book, the explanation of "one working historian's faith and practice," by an outstanding specialist in the history of Tudor England. He insists on the autonomy of history as a field of study. Its great purpose, as the nineteenth-century founders of professional history maintained, is to deepen our understanding of the past. Elton argues that its methods as well as its aims differ significantly from those of social science. He offers much practical advice on how to conduct research, how to write history, and also how to teach it. His book will appeal more to "conventional" than to "innovative" students of history, but in the words of Hugh Trevor-Roper, "he represents a definite tradition which periodically needs to be restated."

Gilbert, Felix, and Stephen R. Graubard, eds., **Historical Studies Today** (New York: Norton, 1972. $12.00; paperback, $3.95). This symposium offers a comprehensive report on the latest fashions in historical research, by twenty-two American, British, and French scholars. The rise of social and quantitative history, urban history, and psychohistory are all discussed, together with studies of such older fields as political and military history. These essays first appeared in the Winter and Spring, 1971, issues of the scholarly quarterly, *Daedalus*.

Hexter, J. H., **The History Primer** (New York: Basic, 1971. $10.00). Hexter tackles the question of what the historian does when he explains, and how his explanations contrast with those of the scientist. The thought processes of historians are illustrated by accounts of how little boys get muddy pants, the winning of the 1951 National League pennant race, the fall of a skittish suspension bridge, and appropriate bits and pieces from Hexter's own experiences as a historian of early modern England. His main point comes through loud and clear: the historian's most valuable tool is nothing more or less than common sense.

Hughes, H. Stuart, **History as Art and as Science:** *Twin Vistas on the Past* (New York: Harper, 1964. $4.95; Torchbooks paperback, $1.45). The author is a European intellectual historian at Harvard and a scholar with a lively interest in new trends in historical thinking and writing. He bridges the gulf between those who see history primarily as a literary or philosophical craft and those who see it primarily as a social science. Here he ventures thoughts on the relationship of history to anthropology and psychoanalysis; discusses the "sweep of the narrative line"; and defends the study of contemporary history.

Stern, Fritz, ed., **The Varieties of History:** *From Voltaire to the Present* [1956] (2nd ed., New York: World, 1972. Meridian paperback, $4.95). Stern describes his anthology as "a book by historians about history." The editor has ranged widely in his choice of readings, from Voltaire on the usefulness of history to Theodor Mommsen on the training of historians, and from the "New History" of Robinson and Beard to Nazi and Soviet views of history. Only practicing historians are represented. The collection compensates for its rather loose structure by the freshness and variety of its readings. Many had never before been translated into English.

Tholfsen, Trygve R., **Historical Thinking**: *An Introduction* (New York: Harper, 1967. $7.50; paperback, $5.50). Most of Tholfsen's book is devoted to a history of Western historical thought and writing, from the Greeks and the Old Testament to Ranke and Fustel de Coulanges. The author also discusses contemporary definitions of history. In the chapters on the history of history, he shows that "the historical mode of understanding," the perception of how events are conditioned by their historical context, did not appear until the late eighteenth and early nineteenth centuries. The historian's acute sensitivity to "time-bound uniqueness," in Tholfsen's view, sharply distinguishes his work from that of the social scientist.

2. The Structure of World History

Anyone planning to study or teach history will profit from knowing something about the nature of his discipline, but world history poses special problems. For all of us, world history seems too big to manage. As James Harvey Robinson once wrote, it "includes every trace and vestige of everything that man has done or thought since first he appeared on the earth." Every heartbeat of every human being who has ever lived, every dream, every whisper, every sneeze belongs.

Above all, the student or teacher of world history needs what I might call a "handle." He needs a working view of the over-all structure of world history, a view that allows him to organize his study and sort out his facts. He may acquire his handle from a discipline other than history. He may or may not accept it as true in any ultimate sense. He may eventually discard it, or use it in combination with two or three alternative working views.

In any event, he needs such things, because no one can study all of world history all at the same time. We must have a plan of operations, a way of getting hold of our subject and scaling it down to our human limitations. In much smaller fields, such as American history, this may not be such a problem. But when it is a question of universal history—hundreds of nations living or dead; scores of civilizations and cultures, living or dead; six continents; at least six thousand years—the situation is very different. We need handles.

Let me illustrate. Here are ten possible ways of structuring your study of world history. Each is self-sufficient, or may be combined with one or more others, as you prefer. Some are old, some are recent. Some are better, I believe, than others—but this is a matter of private judgment. Anyone can think of several other possible structures, if he puts his mind to it. The point is: what might work for you, for someone with your special interests and beliefs?

1. *The Hand of Providence.* If you are a professing Jew, Christian, or Muslim, you must consider the possibility that the founders of your faith, and all the many universal historians who have taken inspiration from them, offer the only true account of the meaning and structure of world history. In terms of the Western revealed religions, history is the unfolding of a providential plan for the human race, a time of testing, a time of struggle between good and evil, and a time blessed by divine interventions which result in miracles, revelations, and (for Christians) the appearance on earth in corporeal form of God himself. Faith-professing historians such as Herbert Butterfield argue that the scholar should avoid the introduction of religious value judgments into his professional work. Certainly in a secularized age,

like our own, and in a country whose constitution decrees separation of church and state, like the United States, Butterfield's advice is easy to take. But is it good advice—for the believer? At least in the privacy of your home or office there is no reason why you should not see world history in terms of your faith. Judaism, Christianity, and Islam are all religions with an intense historical consciousness; they claim to know the meaning of world history; any believing historian can find in the articles of his faith a structure into which he can fit all that he has learned or will ever learn.

2. *What Goes Up Must Come Down.* Even more ancient, perhaps, than the providential theory of history is the cyclical theory. The belief that states inevitably rise and fall was common in antiquity throughout the world. Christians refused to apply it to "sacred" history, but not to the history of the "earthly city." Ibn Khaldun subscribed to a cyclical theory; so did Machiavelli and Vico and Oswald Spengler. In form this is more a sociological theory than a historical one, but historians can make use of it, especially since no one is likely to insist that every new turn of the wheel must take exactly the same amount of time and happen in exactly the same way. The spectacle of great empires soaring and crashing—whether Roman, Byzantine, Persian, Turkish, Mongol, Chinese, British, or any other—has a perennial fascination for students of history. Nor is there any reason to confine the application of cyclical theory to politics. It can also be used to explain economic life, the arts, church history, and, as in Spengler's work, the growth and decay of whole civilizations, viewed as organisms.

3. *Good Tidings.* The idea of progress has suffered some hard knocks in the twentieth century, but many people still believe that history records the gradual improvement of mankind, or some significant portion of mankind, through the centuries. One man's "progress," of course, is often another man's "decline." Everything depends on his idea of what is good. For this

purpose, criteria must be imported from outside historical study. One may, for example, attach supreme importance to the development of science and technology, and see this as constituting progress. Or he may stress the growth of personal freedom and social justice. Or he may trace progress along many lines simultaneously. All that matters is the discovery of a generally upward moving curve in history from an early age judged inferior to a modern age judged measurably better, when everything is taken into account. For the believer in progress, this is the meaning of historical experience. His belief tells him what to look for in history and what use to make of it. At the same time, he runs the risk of finding certain ages or cultures "dark" and "unimportant" because they seem to contribute nothing to "progress."

4. *The Golden Thread*. Without necessarily endorsing a theory of general progress, the student may elect to center his view of world history on the development of a single idea, institution, or activity of unusual significance to him. A classic example is Benedetto Croce's reading of history "as the story of freedom." For Croce the perennial struggle of mankind for liberty was a golden thread running through the fabric of history, redeeming every age—even the most tyrannous. This thematic approach works well only if the theme chosen is common to all past societies and touches many different aspects of life. Other examples might be "man and the environment," "class struggle," "priests and bureaucrats," "the idea of the good life."

5. *The Ages of Man*. Another structural idea, which may readily be combined with others, is the division of world history into two or more great chronological eras. Again, progress is not necessarily implied. Lewis Mumford in *The Transformations of Man* (1956) discovers five ages of man: nomadic, agrarian, civilized, spiritualized, and mechanized. Karl Marx also discovered five: the ages of primitive communism, personal slavery, serfdom, wage slavery, and future communism. Auguste Comte di-

vided history into theological, metaphysical, and positive ages, dominated by religion, philosophy, and science, respectively. The Christian calendar which reckons forward and backward from the birth of Christ and the traditional terms "ancient," "medieval," and "modern" are also attempts to give structure to universal history. Systems of periodization are inevitably somewhat arbitrary, but they can help the student organize his work.

6. *Compare and Contrast.* One of the latest fashions in the writing of history is "comparative history." Its object is to delineate and explain similarities and differences between comparable societies or between comparable elements in the life of those societies. One may understand the French Revolution better, for example, if he compares and contrasts it with the English, American, and Russian Revolutions, as Crane Brinton did in his book *The Anatomy of Revolution* (1938). Comparative method also has applications in world history. The student may attempt to discover the "essential" character or spirit in each of the major world civilizations and then study each of these "essences" comparatively. Pushed in one direction, comparative history becomes sociology. But if the emphasis falls on the identification of differences, rather than similarities, and if comparative studies are used to further understanding of individual societies rather than to work out universal societal "models," then the comparative method can prove both exciting and historiographically authentic.

7. *Interaction.* Another fruitful approach, which avoids the distortions involved in trying to compare whole civilizations, is the study of contacts between nations and civilizations in space and time. Here the student focuses not on internal development but on concrete historical interaction: how, for example, Indian civilization actually affected Chinese; how Greece and Rome "lived again" during the European Renaissance; how the cultures of Europe were exported to the Americas, with the inevitable sea-changes. Not quite all of world history will be il-

luminated by such a strategy, since the historical connections be-tween certain societies (relatively isolated in space or time) and the rest of mankind are tenuous at best. But it is a thoroughly his-torical-minded strategy, used to good effect by both Arnold J. Toynbee and William H. McNeill.

8. *Great Men.* World history does not reduce to the lives of a few transcendental heroes. But some men and women have obviously changed the course of events more than others, and the biographical view of history has its value. Great Men not only transform their times: they also reflect them, since it seems un-likely that anyone not capable of articulating the ideas and con-cerns of his age could become historically "great." One can also sample not-so-great men as he travels through the past, per-sonalities of modest accomplishment who help to explain the continuity of history. The biographical approach has the advan-tage of permitting one-to-one empathetic contact with the past. We see history in terms of living human beings, not faceless abstractions.

9. *Great Forces.* The advantages and disadvantages of building one's study of world history around biographies are re-versed in the "Great Forces" approach, which deals with masses of men and the tidal pull of their pooled energies. Practitioners of the Great Forces view of history tend to be fatalists, as students of the Great Men tend to believe in free will. History becomes the story of "science," "religion," "the bourgeoisie," "Great Power rivalry," "democracy," "the eternal feminine." The trick is to keep one's list of forces relatively short and to guard against woolly-mindedness.

10. *The Idea of Mankind.* Finally, there is a way of structuring world history that seems especially relevant in an age of planetization and planetary peril: the mankind approach. His-tory can be viewed quite simply as the biography of *Homo sapiens,* taking full account of all the uniqueness of given situa-

tions, group conflicts, cultural differences, and everything else that has divided humankind, but taking full account also of the gradual historical integration of our species, as a world community evolves out of the localized communities of the past. In blood and spirit, mankind has always been a single family. The mankind approach defines history as the process by which the biological and spiritual unity of *Homo sapiens* is translated into sociocultural unity.

The books that follow are studies of world history by a variety of writers, including professional historians, scholars in other fields, and inspired amateurs. Each makes use of one or more of the structural ideas sketched above.

• Cameron, Kenneth Neill, **Humanity and Society:** *A World History* (Bloomington, Ind.: Indiana U. P., 1973. $12.50). A noted Shelley scholar who teaches English at New York University, Cameron reports that he wrote *Humanity and Society* in his spare time, as "a welcome antidote to specialization." His book is a compact interpretative history of mankind from its subhuman origins to the era of the French and American Revolutions. Cameron uncovers a pattern of socioeconomic development from primitive foodgathering to a more or less universal "feudalism" to modern capitalism, now already in decline. World history is not "a senseless welter of brutalities" but the progressive liberation of mankind, as each socioeconomic system plays its appointed part and yields in turn to a higher system. Although Cameron regards cultural evolution as secondary to socioeconomic, he has much to say about the cultural life of each society that he analyzes, and quotes liberally from its literature. This is an unusual, clearly written, and provocative book.

Löwith, Karl, **Meaning in History:** *The Theological Implications of the Philosophy of History* (Chicago: U. of Chicago Press, 1949. $6.50; Phoenix paperback, $1.95). Löwith's book is an interesting illustration of the technique of "reverse chronology." His theme is the way in which modern ideas of world history as progress evolved (mistakenly, he feels) from the Christian belief in divine providence and the Christian hope of a heavenly reward. But he tells his story backward, beginning with such nineteenth-century thinkers as Jacob Burckhardt and Karl Marx and retreating, century by century, to St. Augustine and the biblical view of history. Löwith takes a dim view of modern man and modern secular thought.

McNeill, William H., **The Rise of the West:** *A History of the Human Community* (Chicago: U. of Chicago Press, 1963. $15.00; Phoenix paperback, $4.25). Winner of the National Book Award in History and Biography for 1964, McNeill's *The Rise of the West* is described by Arnold J. Toynbee as "the most lucid presentation of world history in narrative form that I know." Certainly no one should attempt to teach world history nowadays without having read this book. Although in "narrative form," it imposes on world history a clearly defined structure.

McNeill divides the history of civilization into three eras, "The Era of Middle Eastern Dominance to 500 B.C.," "Eurasian Cultural Balance, 500 B.C. to 1500 A.D.," and "The Era of Western Dominance, 1500 A.D. to the Present." He adopts the "diffusionist" thesis that civilization began in Mesopotamia and was diffused eastward and westward from this center in the four millennia before Christ. Independent local development had its part, especially in the most remote of the major Eurasian civilizations, the Chinese; but without the Mesopotamian stimulus, world history as we know it could not have happened. For the two thousand years between 500 B.C. and 1500 A.D., the "Eurasian ecumene" then reached an equilibrium, with its four regional centers (Hellenic, Middle Eastern, Indian, and Chinese) engaged in ceaseless interaction. Finally, after 1500, Western European civilization upset this equilibrium and began to Westernize the globe, a process not yet completed but obviously far advanced. McNeill's thesis forces him to pay scant attention to pre-Columbian America; he is also weak in the area of Latin American history. He concludes that at least in terms of power—technological, scientific, institutional, and artistic—mankind has made great progress. "Men some centuries from now," he writes, "will surely look back upon our time as a golden age."

A shorter version of *The Rise of the West,* specially written to serve as a college text, is available under the title **A World History** [1967] (2nd ed., New York: Oxford U. P., 1971. $15.00; paperback, $5.95).

Manuel, Frank E., **Shapes of Philosophical History** (Stanford: Stanford U. P., 1965. $4.75; paperback, $1.95). A leading scholar in the field of modern European intellectual history, Manuel has written what is certainly the best recent discussion of Western man's attempts to divine the structure of universal history. Unfailingly erudite and witty, *Shapes of Philosophical History* is a series of seven guest lectures given at Stanford University. It traces the history of "philosophical history" from the Greeks and the Book of Daniel through the Middle Ages to Kant, the French Enlightenment, German idealism, and our contemporary age of anxiety. Manuel argues that there are basically only two structural models: the cyclical and the progressive. Western man has shifted uneasily back and forth between the two, "but neither has ever dominated the European intellectual field without the presence in some form of its rival."

Muller, Herbert J., **The Uses of the Past:** *Profiles of Former Societies* (New York: Oxford U. P., 1952. $7.95; Mentor paperback, $1.25). Muller is a professor of literature turned historian, who takes what he calls a "tragic" view of history. "All the mighty civilizations of the past have fallen, because of tragic flaws." But they "have also had real grandeur, a glory that survives their fall." In this book, he offers profiles of Byzantium, ancient Israel, classical Greece, imperial Rome, the Middle Ages, both "white" and "red" Russia, and "the timely East." Although he is fascinated by the variety of history, he also finds high significance in the growth of mankind's "power of self-determination, or freedom to make history. . . . Today the future of the open society is wide open, to triumphs or to disasters of a magnitude hitherto undreamed of." What emerges from a careful study of the past is a call to live. Beyond the pursuit of happiness, we must learn from history the "happiness of pursuit."

Mumford, Lewis, **The Transformations of Man** (New York: Harper, 1956; Torchbooks paperback, $2.95). Well known as a literary critic and a specialist in urban problems, Lewis Mumford is also a perceptive student of history. An earlier work (*The Condition of Man*) studied the history of Western civilization from the Greeks to the second World War. In *The Transformations of Man* he takes a wider view of the past. The first six chapters examine—in just 153 pages—the whole course of universal history, emphasizing the periods of crisis when mankind advanced to higher levels of consciousness and social organization. The transitions from animal to human, from hunting to agriculture, from barbarism to civilization, from early civilization to spiritualized civilization, and from antiquity to the modern world of science and technology are painted in broad strokes. In the final chapters, Mumford presents two alternatives for the future: a "post-historic" culture dominated by the logic of the machine or a humanistic "world" culture freely formed by free men.

● Nehru, Jawaharlal, **Glimpses of World History** (New York: John Day, 1942. Reprinted by New York: Asia, $9.00; abridged as **Nehru on World History,** Bloomington, Ind.: Indiana U. P., Midland paperback, $2.45). Between 1930 and 1933, while a political prisoner of the British, the future premier of India wrote this long, rambling sketch of world history, in the form of 196 letters to his young daughter. Nehru was not, of course, a professional historian in any sense, and he leans rather heavily on H. G. Wells's *Outline of History*. But his book is still interesting, for several reasons. It gives insight into the mind of one of the century's greatest leaders. It devotes relatively more space to Indian and East Asian history than Western writers tend to do. Its style is charming. Finally, it illustrates the progressivist interpretation of universal history: "For history teaches us of growth and progress and of the possibility of an infinite advance for man." About two-thirds of the "letters" (chapters) deal with modern history.

● Sédillot, René, **The History of the World**: *In Three Hundred Pages* [1949] (New York: Harcourt, 1951. Mentor paperback, $0.75). Sédillot gives us a scintillatingly Gallic *survol* ("flyover") of world history. He began, he tells us, with the intention of making economics the axis of his book, but he found that politics had to be brought in as well. Most of the chapters feature a single great nation that the author regards as "preponderant" during the period under discussion. His choices are fairly obvious: the Greeks, the Romans, the Italians, the Spanish, the French, and—since Trafalgar and Waterloo—the Anglo-Saxons. Asia, Africa, and the Americas receive only glancing attention. Sédillot ends on a wry note, condemning the modern religion of progress. In twelve thousand years, man has "undoubtedly learned to live better, but also to kill more efficiently." He has "discovered more about the world and very little about himself."

Spengler, Oswald, **The Decline of the West** [1918–22] (2 vols., New York: Knopf, 1926–28. $10.00 each; abridged by Helmut Werner, New York: Modern Library, $4.95). Planned and partially written before the first World War, *The Decline of the West* was published in Germany in 1918–22. The World War and the unsettled times that immediately followed it encouraged many Europeans and Americans to abandon their faith in unlimited progress and to fear that Western civilization had, indeed, reached the end of its rope. Spengler's book, which seemed to confirm these fears, appeared on the scene at just the right moment. It was an instant success.

It offers an ingenious cyclical theory of world history that finds every society passing through four ages: a springtime of pre-cultural tribalism with a faith based on myth and legend; a high summer of aristocracy and mature religion; an autumn of urban culture dominated by rational philosophy; and a wintertime of cosmopolitan civilization ruled by science and materialism. "Civilization" is for Spengler a term applied only to a society that has entered its last season, its period of decline and disintegration. The Western world, he argued, became a "civilization" in this sense at the end of the eighteenth century. It has some hundreds of years still to live, but its death is inevitable, and it can achieve nothing more in the highest departments of culture. Although he discusses eight societies, he draws most of his illustrations from the histories of just three: the classical, the "Arabian" (the Near East and Byzantium), and the Western (since the fall of Rome). The complete work, in two large volumes, demands patience, but the attractive abridgement by Helmut Werner will meet the needs of most readers.

Stavrianos, L. S., **The World to 1500**: *A Global History* (Englewood Cliffs, N.J.: Prentice, 1970. $8.95). **The World since 1500:** *A Global History* [1966] (2nd ed., Englewood Cliffs, N.J.: Prentice, 1971. $10.95). This is a textbook in two volumes for college world history courses, by a specialist in Balkan history. On the whole, it approaches world history along much the same lines followed by William H. McNeill in *The Rise of the West*. Stavrianos agrees with both McNeill and Franz Boas that the key to human progress is "accessibility and interaction." The most accessible peoples, who have the greatest opportunity to interact with others, "are the most likely to forge ahead." *The*

World to 1500 centers on the major Eurasian civilizations of antiquity and their impact upon one another. *The World since 1500* treats, at greater length, the rise of western Europe to a dominant position in the world. It seeks to explain why western Europeans, and not some other people, "brought together the continents of the world and thus began the global phase of world history." Stavrianos concludes that although Europe has lost its political ascendancy in the contemporary world, it is responsible for the shape of the emergent world civilization; in this sense, the West in our country has triumphed, not declined. See also **Man's Past and Present:** *A Global History* (Englewood Cliffs, N.J.: Prentice, 1971. $8.95; paperback, $6.95), in which Stavrianos covers the same ground in a single volume.

Toynbee, Arnold J., **A Study of History** [1934–61] (2 vols., abridged by D. C. Somervell; New York: Oxford U.P., 1947–57. $8.50 and $7.50. 2 vols., Dell paperback, $2.25 the set). An Oxford-trained historian of ancient Greece, Toynbee was strongly influenced by Spengler's *The Decline of the West.* This book, twelve volumes in the unabridged edition, is an attempt to improve on Spengler's work by studying world history in more detail and by avoiding Spengler's somewhat mystical dogmatism. Toynbee examines a vast amount of evidence from the histories of more than twenty civilizations. He also advances a far greater number of generalizations than Spengler did. Yet his interests are in one sense much narrower; for all practical purposes the only things that really hold his attention are political and military history, on the one hand, and religious history, on the other. He agrees with Spengler in finding a cyclical pattern in the history of civilizations, which he describes in great detail, but disagrees that such a pattern is inevitable. He discovers man's best hope in religion and foresees a possible unified world civilization that will bring the cyclical pattern of the past to an end.

Wagar, W. Warren, ed., **History and the Idea of Mankind** (Albuquerque: U. of New Mexico Press, 1971. $12.00). Sponsored by the Council for the Study of Mankind, *History and the Idea of Mankind* is a symposium on the concept of the unity or kinship of mankind as this concept has developed in some of the world's major cultures. Chapters on Indian, Chinese, Jewish, Islamic, and Western history survey the traditional idea of mankind in each of these areas. Other chapters explore the relationship between the idea of mankind and modern nationalism, science and technology, racial theory, and religion and ideology. The book illustrates the "mankind" approach to the study of world history, discussed earlier in this chapter.

● Wells, H. G., **The Outline of History** [1920] (rev. ed., updated by Raymond Postgate; Garden City, N.Y.: Doubleday, 1971. $9.95). *The Outline of History* is the work of a novelist with a lively interest in social problems. He came to believe that the first World War was in part the result of the narrowly national teaching of history that prevailed in European schools before 1914. The obvious antidote to this teaching, he maintained, was to revive the tradition of universal history. H. G. Wells not only had much to do with its revival in our century: he also wrote the most commercially successful history book of his generation, a book that sold more than a million copies in its first decade. World history, for Wells, was both cyclical and progressive. It recorded the struggles of "communities of will" against "communities of obedience"—of open societies against closed ones. At the same time, Wells noted a steady increase in the size of communities and in their interaction, tending inexorably toward the consolidation of mankind in a single world civilization. Wells's book by no means reflected the latest historical research of his own time; it is still more dated today. But the man could write, and his leading ideas are still relevant.

3. Teaching Strategies

The sheer size of world history presents special problems to the teacher. Anyone can acquire a reasonable understanding of the main currents of world history if he works at his own speed, for as long as it takes. Teaching other people to acquire a similar understanding in a one-year high school or college course is something else again. The teacher must practice radical economies.

Some economies are better than others. Turning the world history course into a course in anthropology, for example, or geography, or political science, may make for easier teaching, but it will not be history. I have already spelled out my objections to this "solution." Nor can you dodge the problem by turning world history into Western history. Ever since world history became a major subject in American secondary schools in the 1920's (and two-thirds of them still offer world history as an elective or required course), weary teachers have resorted to this dodge in large numbers. When made available, the college course in world history tends to be an authentically global course, but all too often college history departments shy away from offering world history at all. Their standard freshman survey course is truthfully packaged as "Western Civilization."

But nothing can be called world history that ignores the majority of the world's peoples. Even if we believe, with William H. McNeill, that "the rise of the West" is the upshot of world history, we cannot do justice to our subject when we fail to muster a genuine interest in all the other civilizations that have contributed to the "success" of the West—civilizations that until a few hundred years ago equaled or surpassed the West in military and economic power, to say nothing of their less tangible achievements. It would be no less foolish to imagine that the place of world history could be filled by a course in the "non-Western civilizations." Omitting the West or viewing it as an alien enemy distorts the reality of world history as badly as the conventional Western approach. The world is a big place. We cannot shrink it to suit our prejudices, save at the prohibitive cost of falsifying the past.

Yet even limiting oneself to Western civilization is probably better than the mindless interminable chronicle that some teachers call world history. They take as their duty the stuffing of their students with as many chronologically ordered facts about the human past as they can stuff. Sequences of Caesars and popes are not made any more comprehensible by adding to the Western examples their counterparts in China or India. Cataloguing the books of the Bible or the plays of Shakespeare is not improved by cataloguing the suras of the Koran or the poems of Li Po.

Be sure of this: you cannot present all the facts of world history in one year. Worse yet, you could not present them all if your course lasted a hundred years and met every day. Long ago, when critics attacked H. G. Wells's *Outline of History* on the ground that no one could possibly treat universal history in a single book, Hilaire Belloc pointed out that a perfectly legitimate history of mankind could be written on a single page. He was right. Depending on the principles of selection employed, the writer or teacher of world history can deal with his subject at any length he likes. He will never exhaust his subject, but the amount of space or time he allots to his task is purely arbitrary.

One simple recommendation that I can offer you is to teach world history in terms of your own preferred thesis about the structure of world history. You could do much worse. This may be politically unwise in some cases, or unduly authoritarian on your part; but any of the ten structures suggested in the previous section can be adapted to the classroom. How much better, for example, to teach history as the "story of freedom" or the "march of progress" or the "hand of providence" than to teach it as an indigestible mass of miscellaneous facts!

It is perhaps a still better idea to build a course that gives the student opportunity to choose for himself how he will interpret world history. Expose him to a variety of structures, if you can. Help him to see that history is a subject that demands creative thought far more than it demands a prodigious memory. One gambit in the world history course, therefore, can be a frank acknowledgment on your part, as a teacher, that there are many ways of organizing the study of the past. Why not take your students into your confidence and admit the Awful Truth? You might also seize this opportunity to explain your own particular point of view (if you have one). The beauty of this gambit is that your students can discuss answers to the question of how to structure world history without "knowing" very much history at all. At the same time, they can be developing hypotheses that they will want to test as the year progresses. Problems will begin forming in their minds, with solutions already half-framed; and whatever we may think about the danger of leaping to conclusions, I am afraid that most of us learn more by leaping than by plodding.

A gambit is not the whole chess game. What happens next? Clearly, there are dangers in keeping all ends open and all issues up in the air. You will have to select a structure for your course: topics that you want to explore, which are manageable with the materials at your disposal and the students you happen to have. Unless you are so strongly committed to a single thesis about the meaning and mechanism of history that no other possibility exists for you, the best formula for organizing a course is to bring a variety of approaches together under one roof—whether or not they are logically compatible. Approaches that do harmonize, such as the study of the interaction of civilizations and the comparative method, can be used at the same time. Others will have to be used at different times. But there is no reason why a course has to proceed with terrifying predictability along the same lines month after month to the bitter end.

Whatever you do, I suggest that you often return to the psychology of your opening move: in other words, cast most of your topics in the form of problems to be solved, not litanies to memorize. The most fashionable word in social studies education today is "inquiry," and this is one fashion that I cannot praise too highly. It does not necessarily mean digging out answers exclusively from primary sources. But it does mean an attempt to bring into the classroom the inquiring spirit of the scholar-historian as he sets about his work. "History," in Greek, was the word for "investigation." The historian is a man who is curious about events, and who seeks to explain how and why they happened. If the questions are not in his mind, he may as well give back his degrees and go fishing.

In this connection, I think it is unfortunate that so many world history courses begin with the Sumerians. How many students whether in tenth grade or the sophomore year of college arrive in September buzzing with questions about Sumer? They may not be able to name a single city in China or a single country in Central America, and we want them to care desperately about Sumer!

The place to begin a study of the past is not the beginning, but the present day. Start with the questions that already exist in the minds of your students, or that you can put there with a minimum of agony. Why is Germany divided? Why is India less industrialized than Japan? Why do the Russians live under a socialist form of government and economy? Why do many Latin Americans fear and resent their Yankee neighbors? Why is the world overpopulated? Answering these questions will require at least a step or two backward into time. If you like, you can play the reverse chronology game indefinitely, although it may become a bit tedious after a while. For example: the postwar settlement that explains the division of Germany raises the question of why there was a war in the first place. The ambitions of Hitler raise the question of why the Weimar Republic failed to work. The Weimar Republic raises the question of how and why Germany lost, and mankind fought, the first World War. Ultimately, we find ourselves back in the Bronze Age.

This may be wretched excess. But at least to begin a course with present-day problems makes good sense. Take the student as you find him and work first on the questions that already grip his attention. The answers to these questions will raise others. The supply is never exhausted.

Virtually all matters of interest to the historian can be framed as problems that cry for solution. As a teacher of world history, you will probably find it a good rule of thumb to pose problems that have origins deep in the past and encompass the life not just of nations or even of civilizations, but of all civilizations. Begin with present-day questions such as the struggle in Northern Ireland or the Arab threat to Israel. Either problem can lead you back to an exploration of the history of religion. You can compare and contrast the religions of mankind in world-historical perspective. You can discuss the role of religions in warfare and international power politics. Have men ever before fought in the name of religion to secure political advantages, and if so, how and why? It would not be difficult to spend half a semester on the problem of the historical relationship between religion, politics, and war.

Then devote another half-semester to the problem, for example, of how nations have succeeded, or failed, in the attempt to build industrial economies. The interplay of ideology, economics, and technology is a fascinating one—especially when you can study how matters have actually worked out in actual countries. Perhaps you will also want to answer the question of how the traditional agricultural economy that nations now seek to transform replaced primitive hunting and subsistence farming thousands of years ago. What parts did religion, women, slavery, education, and bureaucracies play in all this? How did the Chinese experience differ from the Greco-Roman, or the Arab? Why did the West apparently gain such a far lead over the Asian and African peoples after about 1500?

Focusing on problems such as these means that you risk losing touch with the narrative flow of history. I see nothing wrong with varying the pace of a world history course by requiring a certain amount of narrative reading or offering lectures in the narrative style. Often such materials can throw light on the very problems that you are trying to solve. A well told story also has great entertainment value. It provides badly needed recreation for fagged minds. But a course that consists of nothing but narrative kills curiosity and removes the student from any active role in the knowledge-seeking process.

Doing interpretative issues also means that you may not "cover" all the ground usually prescribed in model world history curricula. Whatever approach you choose, your students can do no more than establish a few beachheads on the vast continent of world-historical learning: there is only so much time in one year. It is far better to make these beachheads safe and strong, captured by active thought, by strenuous adventures of the mind, than to wander aimlessly over the whole terrain and gain no hold at all.

If you have a strong interest in the social sciences, another helpful strategy is to devote part of your course to a testing against historical evidence of the generalizations of these sciences. What can we learn from the economist's laws of the business cycle, from the anthropologist's theories of cultural diffusion, from the political scientist's models of international relations? Do civilizations really rise and fall according to a predictable pattern, as many sociologists and sociologically-minded historians have argued?

Also, do not overlook the help you can receive from scholars in the humanities. Art and music history, the study of literature, philosophy, comparative religions, and history of science and technology are fields with just as much relevance to history and history teaching as any of the social sciences. I mean this quite literally. History is the study of existential man, not political man or economic man or social man. Existential man, before all else, is the full man, a thinker and dreamer as well as a struggler for power or a seeker of status. There is something of the artist, philosopher, scientist, and prophet in each of us, and in all our societies. A painting can tell us as much about its society as a constitution. An epic poet or a novelist can reveal the life of his time just as effectively as a stockbroker or a field marshal. Even if works of art and thought told us nothing about prevailing social realities and had no influence upon them—which are obviously mad assumptions—they have a self-sufficient importance, as spiritual events in the life of mankind. An idea is just as "factual" as a battle, although it occurs in a different dimension of human experience.

It follows that the teacher of world history (if he has any interest or talent along such lines at all) should cultivate an awareness of man as a seeker of truth and beauty. He has an obligation to his students, not just to decorate his course with an occasional filmstrip session, but to make slides, films, recordings, play and poetry readings, and multi-media shows an integral part of the learning experience in his world history classroom. He should assign novels and other literary material as freely as he assigns government documents and the memoirs of statesmen.

I shall go a step further. A world history course can be devoted almost in its entirety to cultural history. No one would raise an eyebrow if you spent all your time on politics and economics. Why should they protest if you spend most of it on literature and art and philosophy? Are these not part of mankind's history? Are they not central to the human condition? No doubt a lopsidedly "cultural" course would have grave shortcomings, and my preference is for the kind of course that strikes a good balance among all mankind's activities, just as the ideal course should not dwell too long on any one civilization. But life is short, and the time available for the world history course is shorter still. If you have to economize, you are actually better advised to limit the number of activities of man you teach than to limit your temporal-spatial reach.

Another, and perhaps less dangerous, formula for economizing is to select relatively short periods of time for intensive study, covering the centuries in between by lectures that leap at breakneck speeds. Centering on just a few years in the history of a civilization gives you an opportunity to expose your students to primary source materials and allows them to gain familiarity with alien cultures that hovers always just out of reach when you move at conventional velocities. There is no harm in spending a month, for example, on the world of the fifth century B.C. (the century of Confucius, Buddha, and Socrates), and then ripping through the next four centuries in a day.

But the best "strategy" of all is for you, the teacher, to keep intellectually alive. None of us can learn all we need to know in our college and graduate school days. None of us can remain fresh and vital as teachers unless we take periodic nourishment from the ongoing life of our discipline. Stop reading, and you are dead. You may have only two hours a week that you can devote to "professional growth." Spend them reading. What happens to a stamp collector who stops collecting stamps, because he has "enough"? What happens to a golfer who stops golfing, because he has reached his "limit"? What happens to a concert-goer who stops going to concerts, because he has heard "everything"? Don't fool yourself. If you've stopped reading history, you've stopped being a student of history, and pretty soon you will also stop having anything (except very cold mutton) to teach.

Here are several books and periodicals that deal with the problems of history teaching. Not much is available. Material keyed to the special needs of world history teachers is especially scarce, but you may find these titles helpful.

Ballard, Martin, ed., **New Movements in the Study and Teaching of History** (Bloomington, Ind.: Indiana U.P., 1970. $6.95). Ballard's symposium originated in Great Britain; all but two of the eighteen contributors are British university historians or teachers in secondary schools. Since many Americans are unfamiliar with the British education system, parts of this book may have little value for them, but it is always fascinating to see how educators in a different country cope with problems similar to those encountered here. The world history teacher will be particularly interested in the chapters on "World History in the Schools" by William H. McNeill, "Widening Our Historical Horizon" by Arnold J. Toynbee, and "History and the Social Sciences" by Derek Heater.

● Baxter, Maurice G., Robert H. Ferrell, and John E. Wiltz, **The Teaching of American History in High Schools** (Bloomington, Ind.: Indiana U.P., 1964). Through interviews, visits, and a state-wide questionnaire, the authors (all professors of American history at Indiana University) collected much valuable information about the teaching of American history in the high schools of Indiana. They find that American history is, on the whole, very poorly taught in our secondary schools. The chief source of the trouble in their judgment is the unbookishness and anti-intellectualism of the school environment, which produces teachers who have no professional commitment to their discipline: in short, teachers who do not read history. One conclusion is that history departments in colleges and universities must resume the leadership role in preparing teachers that they have too often surrendered to educationists. Although the authors do not discuss the teaching of world history, their research and recommendations should be of interest to any social studies teacher.

Engle, Shirley H., ed., **New Perspectives in World History** (Washington: National Council for the Social Studies, 1964. $6.00; paperback, $5.00). This is a massive collaborative effort to outline recent trends in the interpretation of world history for the benefit of classroom teachers. The first three parts, by academic specialists, discuss interpretative trends in intellectual history, period history, and the study of world regions. The authors include many useful references to new books in each field. In Part Four, educators and historians offer "New Perspectives in the Study and Teaching of World History." Included are Shirley H. Engle's argument for the building of a model of human social behavior as the function of world history; an inventory of other disciplines that can enrich the study of history by Daniel F. McCall; practical suggestions for organizing a world history course by Edith West (with some further thoughts on the same topic by two leading historians, Joseph R. Strayer and L. S. Stavrianos); and an essay on inquiry by Byron G. Massialas. The thirty-three essays in this well planned symposium vary in quality, but it is a work of almost heroic proportions.

• Fenton, Edwin, **The New Social Studies** (New York: Holt, 1967. Paperback, $4.10). Fenton's name is well known to secondary school teachers as the author, editor, or director of several innovative classroom texts and curriculum projects in the social studies. He has also written a college methods text, **Teaching the New Social Studies in Secondary Schools:** *An Inductive Approach* (New York: Holt, 1966. $11.00). In this much shorter work, he discusses the objectives of the "new" social studies and shows how these objectives may be reached through improved teaching strategies, classroom materials, pupil deployment, and teacher preparation. Fenton is a believer in the inquiry approach to social studies teaching, but he also insists that inquiry skills developed by students should be used to equip them with the knowledge of society and history they need to function intelligently as good citizens. A Harvard-trained historian, the author displays a special sensitivity to the humanistic values of historical study.

The History Teacher (Long Beach, Calif., 1967–). Founded by Leon Bernard of Notre Dame University, this is a quarterly journal devoted to the needs and interests of the teaching profession. It includes articles on new interpretations of history, reports on innovations in teaching, and reviews of printed and audio-visual classroom materials. In 1972 the journal moved from its former home at Notre Dame to California State University at Long Beach.

Massialas, Byron G., and C. Benjamin Cox, **Inquiry in Social Studies** (New York: McGraw, 1966. $9.65). Massialas and Cox are social studies educators with strongly anti-historical leanings. Because contemporary society is experiencing rapid change and conflict at all levels, they argue that the task of the schools is to "assume a role of creative reconstruction." The goal of education "should be the reflective examination of values and issues of current import." The social studies classroom should become a "forum of inquiry," where students through the use of social science methodology produce "a body of tested principles and generalizations about human relations and societies." In the authors' view, history—or at least traditional "narrative-descriptive" history—has dominated the social studies curriculum far too long. Undue deference has also been given to history in the training of social studies teachers. History can supply students with useful data and case studies, but Massialas and Cox assign top priority in the curriculum to the social sciences.

Social Education (Washington, 1937–). This is a successful and innovative journal for high school teachers and educationists in the social studies field. Its first editor, Erling M. Hunt, expounded its continuing philosophy in the first issue (January, 1937): "We recognize that, while some specialization is necessary to competence, nevertheless history, geography, government, economics, sociology, and social psychology are, in the schools, all fundamentally one, all concerned with the study of man and society." *Social Education* often publishes articles of special concern to teachers of history. Unfortunately, it is as little known among university historians as *The American Historical Review* is among high school teachers.

The Social Studies: *A Periodical for Teachers and Administrators* (Philadelphia, 1909–). The history of this journal tells a good deal about the changing relations between history and the social sciences, and between university historians and secondary school teachers. It began in 1909 as *The History Teacher's Magazine.* The first issues featured articles by such outstanding university scholars of the time as George Burton Adams, Charles H. Haskins, C. H. McIlwain, and Frederick Jackson Turner. In 1918 it became *The Historical Outlook: A Journal for Readers and Teachers of History and the Social Studies.* The title was changed to *The Social Studies* in 1934, with an announcement that henceforth much greater attention would be paid to the social sciences. Over the years, the university historians have gradually disappeared from its pages, and it has become a journal for high school teachers and educationists exclusively.

West, Edith, ed., **Improving the Teaching of World History** (Washington: National Council for the Social Studies, 1949). Unlike the later N.C.S.S. symposium edited by Shirley H. Engle (reviewed above), this one stresses teaching strategies. Most of the contributors are secondary school teachers and professors of education. The chapters are brief and sharply focused.

After surveys of the status of world history teaching in America and abroad, the authors present suggestions for curriculum development; alternative ways of structuring the high school course in world history (chronological, topical, the area studies approach, the current affairs approach); the learning of time and place concepts; projects and activities for the world history course; and a review of printed and audio-visual materials. In addition, six chapters by historians and social scientists explore interpretative trends in such fields as geography, anthropology, and social history. Much of the material in the symposium is now woefully dated, but the teacher can still benefit from its practical ideas.

chapter	Reference
two	Tools

1. Guides to Reading and Research

You have often heard the truism that what matters in scholarship is not knowing something, but knowing where to find it. If the truism is true, we are in trouble! Many teachers and almost all students, up to and including doctoral candidates, really have no idea "where to find it." Thirteen years after earning my Ph.D., I still did not know or had not ever used quite a few of the reference tools discussed below, when I started work on *Books in World History.*

Our task in this chapter is to survey some of the reference materials that students and teachers of history should know. These are works that could help you in finding books, in writing term papers, in preparing lectures and other classroom happenings, or in doing research for publication.

One valuable aid is the research handbook, usually intended for use as a text in college historiography courses. The "classic manual on all aspects of research and writing" (so say the publishers) is Jacques Barzun and Henry F. Graff, **The Modern Researcher** [1957] (rev. ed., New York: Harcourt, 1970. $8.50; paperback, $3.75). The publishers' description does not, for once, seem far off. *The Modern Researcher* is a comprehensive guide to the writing of history, from asking the first questions through fact-finding and verification to the rules of citation. The authors include a long bibliography of reference works.

A book such as Barzun and Graff's contains some material that will obviously be useless to you unless you plan to write history yourself. But no great gulf yawns between the mental processes involved in writing history and those involved in studying and teaching it. In fact, this is what the "inquiry" method now popular in social studies education is all about. The mind-set of the "inquirer" is also the mind-set of the "researcher." In both cases you are not content simply to tell or hear ready-made stories about the past. You are asking questions and trying to solve problems. Studying in detail how historians write history can make you a far more intelligent and sophisticated reader of history—and a better teacher.

A little older than Barzun and Graff, but also available in an updated second edition, is Louis Gottschalk's **Understanding History:** *A Primer of Historical Method* [1950] (2nd ed., New York: Knopf, 1969. $4.95; paperback, $3.50). Unlike *The Modern Researcher,* which stresses writing, Gottschalk's book devotes most of its chapters to such topics as the objectives of historians, the nature of historical sources, and theories of history. It has relatively more to say, in other words, about the interpretation of sources than about the composition of historical essays; but either book will help guide you through the reference literature and the kinds of sources available to the historian.

Yet another sort of guidebook is **How to Study History,** by Norman F. Cantor and Richard I. Schneider (New York: Crowell, 1967. Paperback, $2.95). The authors' main purpose is to help undergraduates wrestle with their everyday problems: reading primary and secondary sources, writing examinations and term papers, using the library. Chapters such as "The Materials of History," "A Practical Lesson in How to Read a History Book," and "Research Techniques" have much to offer anyone interested in improving his familiarity with the basic tools of his trade.

All the foregoing are full-length books. A considerably shorter work of great practical value is Wood Gray et al., **Historian's Handbook:** *A Key to the Study and Writing of History* [1959] (2d ed., Boston: Houghton, 1964. Paperback, $2.95). In addition to chapters in outline form on the nature of history and the writing of historical papers, Gray provides in his second chapter ("Pursuit of Evidence") a convenient and yet very extensive list of research tools in all the fields of world history. Hundreds of library catalogues, bibliographies, periodical and newspaper indexes, reference works, and atlases are listed, with full bibliographical information. If you want to know where to find a place that will tell you "where to find it," consult *Historian's Handbook.*

So much for the guidebooks. If you do not need them, you are ready to move on to a different category of reference tool: the scholarly bibliography. The book you are now reading is such a work, although far less comprehensive than the best professional efforts in this field. Nothing in the English language remotely compares with **Guide to Historical Literature** [1931] (new ed., New York: Macmillan, 1961. $16.50), a project of the American Historical Association, edited by George Frederick Howe and others. Nearly a thousand pages in length, the *Guide* covers all kinds of history, and most of the twenty thousand entries are discussed in paragraph-long notes. Included are lists of reference works, books on history teaching, and general studies of world history since the earliest times. The chief drawback of the *Guide* in the 1970's is its age—bibliographies age even more rapidly and more disastrously than movie starlets. It covers the literature of world history only down to 1956, with a few entries on works published between 1956 and 1960, when it went to press. For the modern period, see also John Roach, ed., **A Bibliography of Modern History** (New York: Cambridge U. P., 1968. $6.95).

Another excellent guide to the scholarly literature is the American Historical Association's **Pamphlets for Teachers and Students of History.** More than seventy of these pamphlets were published between 1956 and 1970. The greater number are in world, as distinguished from U. S., history, and they offer expert judgment on the books in each field, with special attention to recent interpretative trends. Sample titles: John K. Fairbank, "New Views of China's Tradition and Modernization"; Philip D. Curtin, "African History"; and Bryce Lyon, "The Middle Ages in Recent Historical Thought." It is notorious in the profession that the greatest users of these pamphlets have been doctoral candidates preparing for their comprehensive examinations, not the teachers for whom they were originally designed. In 1972 the A.H.A. announced that the series was being replaced by a new one, **AHA Pamphlets.** The new pamphlets (priced like their predecessors at $1.00 each) will provide short interpretative studies of various periods in American and world history, with less emphasis on bibliographical data than in the original series. The first world history title in this series is Harold J. Grimm's "The Reformation." For further details, write to the American Historical Association, 400 A Street S.E., Washington, D.C. 20003.

The needs of high school students are especially well
● served by **World Civilization Booklist:** *Supplementary Reading for Secondary Schools* (Washington: National Council for the Social Studies, 1968. Paperback, $3.50). It lists and briefly describes 1,240 titles, ranging from light historical fiction for young readers to scholarly monographs.

But of course you do not have to consult books such as these to secure reputable lists of works in world history. Almost any good recent textbook contains a bibliography, and some are quite lengthy. The textbook bibliography may be just as serviceable for your purposes as longer, separately published bibliographical works (like this one!).

2. Encyclopedias and Atlases

If what you want is not reading suggestions but quick access to specific historical data, a number of good reference works are available, tailored to the needs of historians. Some are not well known, or rarely consulted.

Anyone who teaches world history should not only use but own a copy of William L. Langer, ed., **An Encyclopedia of World History** [1940] (5th ed., Boston: Houghton, 1972. $17.50). The 1,569 pages of this one-volume historical encyclopedia probably house more "hard data" about the human past than any book of comparable length ever written. It offers fully indexed chronological lists of principal events in the histories of all parts of the world, with explanatory and interpretative notes, genealogical charts, maps, and other materials. Because of its chronological format, the Langer *Encyclopedia* is obviously a better source for political events than for cultural and economic history, but it contains at least a little of everything. The scholars who collaborated in producing it are of the first rank.

See also **Everyman's Dictionary of Dates** [1911] (6th ed., New York: Dutton, 1971. $6.50). This is actually a dictionary of world history from earliest times, although the alphabetically arranged entries emphasize chronology rather than content. A representative entry is the one on "Nepal," which packs twenty-three dates into a thirty-eight line article.

An "encyclopedia" that is actually not an encyclopedia is John Bowle, ed., **The Concise Encyclopedia of World History** (New York: Hawthorn, 1958). Profusely illustrated, this volume offers a series of essays for the intelligent layman on various segments of world history by twenty-three scholars, mostly of Oxford University, with especially full treatment of the Afro-Asian world. More recently, a team of forty scholars at Columbia University has produced **The Columbia History of the World,** eds. John A. Garraty and Peter Gay (New York: Harper, 1972. $20.00). Its 101 chapters supply the most comprehensive review of world history available in a single volume in narrative form.

In addition to these works, which are strictly historical, you will wish to consult from time to time a variety of other kinds of reference works. I find all standard encyclopedias fairly exasperating, but the **Encyclopaedia Britannica** remains the best of the lot, in English or any other language. Except for contemporary history, you will be well advised to use the out-of-print 11th edition (29 vols., 1911). The social sciences are well represented by two great encyclopedias with almost identical titles: **Encyclopaedia of the Social Sciences** (15 vols., New York: Macmillan, 1930–34); and **International Encyclopedia of the Social Sciences** (17 vols., New York: Macmillan and the Free Press, 1968). The earlier set included historians on its editorial staff; the later one does not. Both contain articles of substantial length on the major social thinkers throughout history as well as on the concepts and branches of the social sciences. But do not confuse them. The second is not a revised edition of the first, but a wholly new production. See also the **Encyclopaedia of Religion and Ethics** (13 vols., New York: Scribner, 1908-26). For brief biographies of the scientists of all periods and countries, see Allen G. Debus, ed., **World Who's Who in Science** (Chicago: Marquis, 1968. $60.00).

The place to go if you want to know the history of a word, as well as its modern meanings, is **A New English Dictionary on Historical Principles** (10 vols. in 13; Oxford: Clarendon, 1888–1928). Four other standard reference works of exceptional value are the **Columbia Encyclopedia** [1935] (3rd ed., New York:

Columbia U. P., 1963. $49.50); **Webster's Biographical Dictionary** [1943] (rev. ed., Springfield, Mass.: Merriam, 1972. $12.95); **Webster's Geographical Dictionary** [1949] (rev. ed., Springfield, Mass.: Merriam, 1969. $9.50); and the **Columbia-Lippincott Gazetteer of the World** (New York: Columbia U. P., 1952. $75.00). The last two mentioned contain not only geographical information and maps but also thumbnail chronologies, especially useful for urban and provincial history.

Finally, you need a reliable historical atlas. Most confine themselves to European history, with the rest of the world covered only as it became involved in European overseas expansion. For world history, nothing is quite so good as **Westermanns Atlas zur Weltgeschichte** (Braunschweig: Westermann, 1956), but you have to read German to use it. An acceptable alternative is R. R. Palmer, ed., **Atlas of World History** (Chicago: Rand, 1957. $8.95), which contains 128 maps, 92 of them in color, each briefly explained in the accompanying text. Palmer's work, as advertised, is a world history atlas; the non-Western civilizations receive adequate treatment. There is also an abridged paperbound
• version of this atlas: Palmer, ed., **Historical Atlas of the World** (Chicago: Rand, 1961. $1.00). The best atlas of modern history (since 1492) is H. C. Darby and Harold Fullard, eds., **The New Cambridge Modern History Atlas** (New York: Cambridge, 1970. $32.50).

3. Multi-Volumed Historical Series

Despite the great cost and unending busy work involved, publishers in all countries from time to time bring out ambitious multi-volumed historical series: scholarly, popular, or documentary. As a rule these are collaborative ventures; and as a rule, the more editors, authors, and consultants are involved, the poorer the overall quality of the venture.

A number of multi-volumed histories of mankind or of

Western civilization have appeared in the last two centuries. They occupy many yards of shelf space in our major libraries. They tend to age almost as rapidly as encyclopedias or bibliographies, and collect more than their share of dust. But some of them are worth knowing about.

Of world histories in English, the best publicized in recent years has been **The History of Mankind** prepared under UNESCO auspices by the International Commission for a History of the Scientific and Cultural Development of Mankind (New York: Harper, 1963–). Planned in six volumes, with four now published, this series has gathered poor reviews. Perhaps it is a case of too many cooks spoiling the broth; or too much international bureaucracy; or the need not to offend the official sensibilities of the U. N.'s member nations; or the untimely death of some of the authors and editors. In any case, *The History of Mankind* has not been an overwhelming critical success. As one reviewer wrote in a recent issue of *The American Historical Review* (commenting on the second volume): "Rarely, if ever, can so many learned men have labored so long on a history to such little purpose. . . . This conglomeration of savants from so many nations could no more have produced a coherent historical synthesis than the builders of the Tower of Babel could have created the Parthenon."

All the same, UNESCO's *History of Mankind* has its values. The first volume (1963), by Jacquetta Hawkes and Sir Leonard Woolley, treats prehistory and the beginnings of civilization. The second, by Luigi Pareti and two assistants, is entitled *The Ancient World: 1200 B.C. to A.D. 500* (1965). The third and fifth volumes are still to come. Volume Four, *The Foundations of the Modern World: 1300–1775* (1970. $20.00), is the work of an American team headed by Louis Gottschalk. Volume Six, *The Twentieth Century* (1967. $18.50), was written by Caroline F. Ware and others. Do not expect dazzling feats of imagination and ingenuity in any of the volumes, but three things at least must be said in favor of this undertaking. It is a noble attempt to bring scholars together in an international dialogue; it is universal, and not just Western, history; and it is useful as a work of reference—both for its text and for its many photographs, drawings, maps, and other visual aids.

The University of Michigan History of the Modern World, ed. Allan Nevins and Howard M. Ehrmann (Ann Arbor, Mich.: U. of Michigan Press, 1958–. $7.50–$10.00 each), approaches world history more conventionally, as a series of national and regional histories. Seventeen volumes are available on the modern history of countries such as Germany, France, Italy, and India, and of regions such as the Far East, the Near East, and Latin America. Each volume is the work of a single author, and most of these are well known senior scholars in their fields—Albert Guérard, Maurice Ashley, C. Hartley Grattan, Percival Spear, to name a few. Unfortunately, the editors are not always judicious in their apportionment of space. For example, Grattan is allowed two volumes to present the history of the Southwest Pacific (essentially Australia and New Zealand), whereas the whole modern history of China, Korea, and Japan is compressed into a single volume.

For a comprehensive multi-volumed history of Western civilization, see the three series published by Cambridge University Press: **The Cambridge Ancient History** (12 vols., 1923–39); **The Cambridge Medieval History** (8 vols., 1913–36. $23.50–$32.50 each); and **The New Cambridge Modern History** (13 vols., 1957–. $19.50 each). The volumes cover given periods in Western history; the individual chapters, each by a different scholar, discuss either a topic in the history of the period or a country or region. The non-Western world figures only in its relationship to the West. Despite the excellence of many chapters here and there, the Cambridge histories lack unity and are difficult to use as works of reference. For the medieval series, a two-volume abridgement is available, Charles W. Previté-Orton, **The Shorter Cambridge Medieval History** (New York: Cambridge U. P., 1952. $28.50).

Better for modern Western history than the Cambridge set is William L. Langer, ed., **The Rise of Modern Europe** (New York: Harper, 1934–. $7.95–$10.00 each). Seventeen volumes have appeared so far in this nearly complete chronological series, each by a different scholar, each stressing trends and topics of continent-wide significance, with well chosen illustrations and excellent bibliographical essays. Scholars of the stature of Crane Brinton, Geoffrey Bruun, Carl J. Friedrich, and Langer himself make this a project of outstanding merit. As a bonus, all the volumes are now available in paperbound editions in the Harper Torchbooks series ($2.25–$4.95 each). Also in paperback, as well as cloth binding, is a British set of unusual graphic beauty,

● **History of Civilization Library,** ed. Geoffrey Barraclough, and published in the United States by Harcourt ($5.50–$7.95 each; paperback, $2.95–$3.95 each). Some twenty titles are in print, written by historians of high international repute. Each book is about two hundred pages long, with more than a hundred illustrations, many in color.

In the realm of popular history, a leading series is Time-

● Life's **Great Ages of Man** (21 vols., New York: Time-Life, 1965–68. $6.95 each), handsomely produced picture-books with brief supporting texts by C. M. Bowra, Basil Davidson, Peter Gay, and other notables. Sprightly prose is the major attraction in another successful work of popular history, Will and Ariel Durant's **The**

● **Story of Civilization** (10 vols., New York: Simon, 1935–67. $10.00–$15.00 each). Except for the first volume, the Durants give us only Western history, and their narrative reaches only as far as the French Revolution, but *The Story of Civilization* has found a large reading public. Scholars prefer to ignore it, since the authors are obviously not professional historians. All the same, this is a work in the grand manner of Voltaire, Macaulay, and Carlyle. It may not quite match these equally "unprofessional" forerunners in depth of vision, but you can read it without having to apologize to anyone.

Another major category of multi-volumed historical works is the "problems" series. Intended for classroom use either in high school or in college, "problems" books select issues in historical interpretation and illustrate the range of opinion by providing excerpts from the scholarly literature on each issue. Sometimes primary sources are included as well. Many of these works are better suited for the teacher's private library or the graduate seminar than for the classroom. But however you use them, they make a valuable contribution to historical thought.

The pioneer series of problems books, which originated at Amherst College in the 1930's, is **Problems in American Civilization,** published by D. C. Heath of Boston. Since this series was launched, Heath has started three others: Ralph Greenlaw and Dwight E. Lee, eds., **Problems in European Civilization;** Edwin Lieuwen, ed., **Problems in Latin American Civilization;** and W. T. de Bary et al., eds., **Problems in Asian Civilizations.** The last two are relatively new, but the Greenlaw-Lee series, which began appearing in 1958, has about sixty volumes in print, all in paperback. Representative titles are Donald Kagan, ed., **Decline and Fall of the Roman Empire:** *Why Did It Collapse?* (1962, $2.25); and Dwight E. Lee, ed., **The Outbreak of the First World War:** *Who or What Was Responsible?* (3rd ed., 1970, $2.25).

Each volume follows the same format: an introduction by the editor, substantial excerpts from ten or twenty scholarly books and articles on the problem at hand, and a bibliographical essay. Sometimes the editors seem to create more controversy than really exists; a few of the volumes go to the other extreme and are quite bland. But on the whole, the editors have done their work well. See also the volumes of the **European Problem Series** published by Holt and the **Major Issues in History Series** published by John Wiley.

In addition to these series, which contain one "problem" per volume, there are several convenient anthologies of problems. One of the newest is Norman F. Cantor and Samuel Berner, eds., **Problems in European History** (3 vols., New York: Crowell, 1971. Paperback, $4.95 each). Brison Gooch, ed., **Interpreting Western Civilization** (2 vols., Homewood, Ill.: Dorsey, 1969. Paperback, $5.05 each) performs the same service, with each chapter edited by a different scholar. Brian Tierney et al., eds., **Great Issues in Western Civilization** [1967] (2nd ed., 2 vols.; New York: Random, 1972. Paperback, $4.95 each) supplies readings from both primary and secondary sources.

The primary sources of world history (need I say?) are almost inconceivably vast, but some valiant editors have plunged into the task of producing comprehensive anthologies in this area as well. They can be helpful either as supplementary reading in the classroom or as reference aids. L. S. Stavrianos has edited a two-volume set, **The Epic of Man to 1500** (Englewood Cliffs, N.J.: Prentice, 1970. $7.95; paperback, $5.95) and **The Epic of Modern Man** [1966] (2nd ed., Englewood Cliffs, N.J.: Prentice, 1971. Paperback, $5.95), intended for use in conjunction with his college world history textbooks. Stavrianos includes a number of excerpts from scholarly sources, but most are primary. See also William H. McNeill et al., eds., **Readings in World History** (10 vols., New York: Oxford U. P., 1968–73. Paperback, $1.50–$2.95 each).

It is no small task to anthologize the primary sources of even one civilization. A major new project is the **Documentary History of Western Civilization,** ed. Eugene C. Black and Leonard W. Levy. Twenty-seven volumes have thus far appeared, with more promised. They are available in paperbound editions published by Harper Torchbooks, at prices ranging from $2.95 to

$4.95 each. For Asia, a good series is W. T. de Bary, Jr., ed., **Sources of Japanese Tradition; Sources of Indian Tradition;** and **Sources of Chinese Tradition** (3 vols., New York: Columbia U. P. 1958–60. $15.00 each; paperback, 6 vols., $2.80–$4.00 each).

4. Journals

I have saved until last a reference aid that is generally used only by specialists, and sometimes not even by them. All branches of scholarship publish journals. In the natural sciences, journals are often more important than books, since scientific research lends itself to presentation in relatively compact forms. A few equations may sum up thousands of hours of work. But in our field, the articles published in journals represent only a small fraction of current research. In fact many scholars subscribe to them because of their reviews and advertisements of recent books and leave the articles unread. More than half the pages of a major journal such as *The American Historical Review* are devoted to reviews, advertisements, letters, lists of recently published books and articles, and the like. Yet this material is vitally important, too. There is no better way of keeping abreast with the scholarly literature in your field than to read the journals.

Not many journals are world history journals. **The American Historical Review,** founded in 1895 and published by the American Historical Association, is one such, and probably the best in the English language. In a recent issue selected at random (June, 1971), the articles dealt with the labor problem in colonial Jamestown, the adolescence of Heinrich Himmler, communism in pre-Marxist France, and the formation of public policy in medieval China. The same issue offered more than 140 signed reviews of books in all fields of history, including books published abroad, and 87 pages listing "other books received" and recently published articles in professional journals. Other countries have comparable journals of broad scope, such as **The English Historical Review** (1886–), but there is nothing else quite like the *A. H. R.* in the United States.

Since 1953 the international commission in charge of preparing the UNESCO *History of Mankind* has also published **The Journal of World History.** The articles in this trilingual journal are by-products of the *History of Mankind* project. Some are good, but the journal, like the rest of the commission's work, does not live up to one's expectations.

Most historical journals are, of course, more specialized than these. In the modern European field, **The Journal of Modern History** (1929–) has little English-language competition. The medieval West is cared for handsomely by **Speculum** (1926–). The history of science has another exceptionally fine journal, **Isis** (1912–). In other branches of world history, see, for example, **The Journal of Asian Studies** (1941–), **The Middle East Journal** (1947–), **The Hispanic American Historical Review** (1918–), and **The Journal of African History** (1960–). All these journals devote a generous portion of each issue to book reviews.

The most painless of historical journals is the British monthly **History Today** (1951–). It offers a variety of illustrated popular (although not necessarily unscholarly) articles in all fields of history. In a recent issue, articles appeared on "Prince Rupert," "The Assassination of Trotsky," "Anti-Slavery and the American Revolution," "Admiral Ushakov: Nelson's Russian Ally," and "Empedocles of Acragas." The issue sported 39 illustrations, some in color, and several book reviews. I hesitate to describe *History Today* as a "reference tool," but it is certainly fun. Since 1967 it has enjoyed brisk competition from a similar American publication, **Mankind.**

chapter
three

The
Ancient
West

At one time, not so many decades ago, nearly all the history studied and taught in the Western world was ancient history. Nowadays, many holders of Ph.D.'s in history have never taken a course or (for all we know) read a single book in the field. The relative decline of ancient history, and also of classical studies generally, sharply distinguishes our generation from earlier periods in the history of scholarship. Nevertheless, very good work is still being done, aided by archeological discoveries of great importance.

The history of the ancient West is simultaneously one of the broadest and narrowest of disciplines. Its breadth is obvious: it includes not only Greece and Rome, but also Judaism and Christianity, the civilizations of Egypt and Mesopotamia, and the empires of ancient Iran. Among these societies are some that arose in the fifth and fourth millennia B.C., long before the emergence of civilization in China and India. But the history of the ancient West is also a narrow field of study, since relatively few of its primary sources have survived. Even such a well documented people as the Greeks are known to us only in bits and pieces: nearly all their art and music and most of their literature and philosophy were lost, probably forever, during the Middle Ages. For example, we have scarcely a tenth of the tragedies known to have been written by Aeschylus, Sophocles, and Euripides. From the hundreds of other tragedians of the fifth century, not one play survives.

Yet we are not speaking of populations remotely comparable to those of modern times. Egypt under Rameses III in the twelfth century B.C. had a total population of perhaps three million. Three hundred thousand people lived in the Athens of Pericles, and even the Roman empire in the age of Augustus Caesar—European, Asian, and African provinces included—had at most one hundred million subjects. The vast majority of these people, needless to say, were in no position to produce any primary sources whatsoever and contributed to mankind's history only their labor, free or slave. That so little remains of what was done by so few prompts many scholars of ancient history to practice extreme caution in drawing interpretative conclusions. It lures others to leaps of speculation that recall the techniques of the historical novelist.

In any event, the more than four thousand years of ancient history in the West have their indispensable place in world history. They are important in their own right; and of course no one can hope to understand medieval and modern Western civilization without a firm grounding in the study of its ancient heritage.

1. The Pre-Classical West

Aldred, Cyril, **Akhenaten, Pharaoh of Egypt** (New York: McGraw, 1968. $10.95). No personality of preclassical Egypt is better remembered than Akhenaten (or Ikhnaton), who reigned during the Eighteenth Dynasty, from 1378 to 1362 B.C. Many writers have argued that his introduction of a new religious cult devoted to the solar disk, Aton, foreshadowed and even helped to influence the monotheistic religion of the ancient Jews. In this new biographical study, Cyril Aldred offers a very different view. Akhenaten, he writes, was far from the revolutionary of modern legend. His ideas "had a strong antiquarian flavor, and attempted to restore the supremacy of the Pharaoh to what it had been in the early Old Kingdom." Neither populist, nor monotheist, nor progressive, Akhenaten used religious "heresy" as a weapon against the classes in Egyptian society that stood in the way of his reactionary ambitions. Aldred supplies a thoughtful analysis of the major interpretative issues. There are also 17 color plates and 120 black and white photographs, which greatly enhance the text.

Bright, John, **A History of Israel** [1959] (2nd ed., Philadelphia: Westminster, 1972. $8.50). Bright traces the religious and political history of Israel from earliest times to the end of the biblical era. Well documented and supplied with color maps and a full index of biblical references, his book is of special value as a guide to the study of the Old Testament. Its theological tendencies are conservative. For a still more conservative but also soundly executed work by a Jewish scholar, see Harry M. Orlinsky, **Ancient Israel** [1954] (2d ed., Ithaca, N.Y.: Cornell U.P., 1960. $5.50; paperback, $1.95).

• Ceram, C. W., **Gods, Graves, and Scholars:** *The Story of Archaeology* [1949] (rev. ed., New York: Knopf, 1967. $8.95; Bantam paperback, $1.95). Since the founding of archeology by J. J. Winckelmann in the eighteenth century, specialists in this dusty discipline have added enormously to our knowledge of the ancient world. The dramatic and human side of their work is highlighted in an engrossing best-seller by Kurt W. Marek, who uses the pen name of C. W. Ceram. He reviews the history of archeological discoveries in Egypt, the Near East, Greece and Italy, and Mexico and Central America. More emphasis falls on the ruins themselves, and the myths and legends surrounding

them, in L. Sprague de Camp and Catherine C. de Camp,
● **Ancient Ruins and Archaeology** (Garden City, N.Y.: Doubleday, 1964. $5.95). The de Camps even include a delightful
chapter on "ruins" that are purely legendary—the lost civilization of Atlantis.

● Childe, V. Gordon, **Man Makes Himself** [1936] (New
York: Mentor paperback, $0.95). A masterpiece of concise in-
terpretation by one of the twentieth century's leading archeologists. Childe surveys all of Western prehistory and ancient history down to about 3000 B.C. from a point of view that blends
Marxism and sturdy Victorian rationalism. He discovers two
great revolutions in this preclassical past: the neolithic revolution, which converted man from a food-gatherer into a farmer
and stockbreeder; and the "urban" revolution, which occurred
first in Mesopotamia, and was made possible by rapid progress
in science and technology. All this involved the exploitation of
some men by other men, but in true Marxist fashion, Childe
views exploitation as a necessary evil, a function of "the dialectics
of progress." Tradition makes the man, he adds, but man in turn
makes (and sometimes breaks) his traditions, so that, in the final
analysis, "man makes himself." See also Jacquetta Hawkes's
excellent contribution to the first volume of the UNESCO *History
of Mankind* [1963], available separately as **Prehistory** (New
York: Mentor paperback, $1.25).

● Cottrell, Leonard, **Life under the Pharaohs** (New York:
Holt, 1960. $5.00; Tempo paperback, $0.75). As a popularizer
of Egyptology, Leonard Cottrell has few rivals. In this little book,
he presents the everyday life of the Egyptians of the Eighteenth
Dynasty (1580–1321 B.C.), the age of Hatshepsut, Thutmose
III, and Akhenaten. Some of the chapters are stories set in the
period. Especially for younger students, *Life under the Pharaohs*
is an excellent introduction to Egyptian social history. Among
● Cottrell's many other books see, for example, **The Lost Phar-**

aohs: *The Romance of Egyptian Archeology* [1951] (Universal paperback, $2.25).

Frankfort, Henri, et al., **The Intellectual Adventure of Ancient Man:** *An Essay on Speculative Thought in the Ancient Near East* (Chicago: U. of Chicago Press, 1946. $8.95; abridged as **Before Philosophy:** *The Intellectual Adventure of Ancient Man,* Penguin paperback, $1.45). This book is "an attempt to understand the view which the ancient peoples of Egypt and Mesopotamia took of the world in which they lived." The authors deplore the conventional tacit assumption "that the Ancients were preoccupied with problems very similar to ours, and that their myths represent a charming but immature way of answering them." Such a view "ignores the gulf which separates our habits of thought, our modes of experience, from those remote civilizations." The opening chapter, by the Dutch scholars Henri and H. A. Frankfort, explores the logic and structure of mythopoeic ("myth-making") thought, demonstrating that it was rooted in a unitary concept of man and nature. Chapters follow on the Egyptian world-view by John A. Wilson and on the Mesopotamian world-view by Thorkild Jacobsen. In a concluding chapter, the Frankforts discuss the transition to a relatively demythologized world-view in Hebrew and Greek thought. There is no better study of how the ancient mind worked.

Kramer, Samuel Noah, **History Begins at Sumer:** *Twenty-Seven Firsts in Man's Recorded History* [1956] (Garden City, N.Y.: Anchor paperback, $1.95). Originally published under the title *From the Tablets of Sumer,* this is the best short introduction to mankind's oldest civilization, established in Mesopotamia in the fifth millennium B.C., long before the founding of the Old Kingdom in Egypt. Kramer tells the story of the Sumerians as a series of "firsts"—the first schools, the first bicameral legislature, the first historian, the first library catalogue, and many others, twenty-seven in all. It is a charming portrait of a long-dead society, written by an able scholar who is also the author of a somewhat more orthodox volume, **The Sumerians:** *Their History, Culture, and Character* (Chicago: U. of Chicago Press, 1963. $7.95; Phoenix paperback, $2.95).

Moscati, Sabatino, **The Face of the Ancient Orient:** *A Panorama of Near Eastern Civilizations in Pre-Classical Times* [1956] (Garden City, N.Y.: Anchor paperback, $2.50). Moscati, a specialist in Semitic studies at the University of Rome, based the present work on a series of radio talks. Like many other books with similar beginnings, *The Face of the Ancient Orient* is boldly conceived, but displays a tendency to oversimplification. The peoples of the ancient Near East are studied in three groups: those of the river valleys (the Sumerians, Babylonians, Assyrians, and Egyptians), who established the first civilized societies; those of the mountains and deserts (the Hittites, Canaanites, Israelites, and others), who acted as "catalysts" in the body social of the old valley empires; and the Persians, also a mountain people by origin, who supplied the final "synthesis" of preclassical antiquity by uniting the entire area under their rule in the sixth century B.C.

Olmstead, Albert T., **History of the Persian Empire** (Chicago: U. of Chicago Press, 1948. Phoenix paperback, $3.95). We forget too easily that Persia (or Iran) is one of the world's oldest empires, founded centuries before the unification of China, and a great power in the ancient world from the time of Cyrus in the sixth century B.C. until the seventh century A.D. Albert T. Olmstead of the Oriental Institute at the University of Chicago gives us in this book a history of the Achaemenid period, from Cyrus to the burning of the capital at Persepolis by Alexander the Great. Political and military history are reinforced by a vivid account of ancient Persian social, economic, and cultural life. Olmstead takes advantage of recent archeological findings in Iran itself, so that he is not wholly dependent, as scholars once were, on biased Greek accounts of the Persian world.

Oppenheim, A. Leo, **Ancient Mesopotamia:** *Portrait of a Dead Civilization* (Chicago: U. of Chicago Press, 1964. $8.50; Phoenix paperback, $3.95). Oppenheim draws a convincing picture of the social and cultural life of two great ancient Mesopotamian peoples, the Babylonians and the Assyrians. He stresses the uniqueness of ancient Mesopotamia, the many ways in which its ideas and institutions differ from those of our modern world. A still older people, the Sumerians, are not included. The author smartly raps some of his colleagues for their tendency to judge dead Asian societies by the standards of Western humanism.

Piggott, Stuart, **Ancient Europe:** *From the Beginnings of Agriculture to Classical Antiquity* (Chicago: Aldine, 1966. $10.00; paperback, $3.95). It is well known that medieval (and hence modern) Europe was much more than a continuation in new dress of the civilization of Mediterranean antiquity. But historians have traditionally paid little serious attention to the other major element in the cultural synthesis of medieval Europe: the contribution of the pre-Celtic, Celtic, and Germanic "natives" who made up the greater part of Europe's population in medieval times.

Stuart Piggott's book is a visually exciting and scientifically penetrating attempt to sum up what archeology can tell us about the last eight thousand years of European prehistory. With the help of 143 line illustrations and 51 plates, the author traces the slow advance of peasant societies across the continent from western Asia, their arts and commerce, their entry into the bronze and iron ages, and their interaction with classical Greece and Rome.

•   Roth, Cecil, **A History of the Jews:** *From Earliest Times Through the Six Day War* [1935] (rev. ed., New York: Schocken, 1970. Paperback, $2.45). The Jewish people have retained their identity through a period of more than three thousand years without—for most of this time—living in a land of their own. Other peoples have survived in spite of foreign rule, in spite of political disunity, in spite of systematic attempts to destroy their culture: the Jews are unique in their survival as a "diaspora," a scattered people residing in many adopted homelands. What holds them together as a people, apart from their religious faith, is their intensely developed historical consciousness. The Bible is the most historically-minded of all sacred texts; it has created a nation whose essence is its history.

Not surprisingly, modern Jewish scholars have written many histories, long and short, of the Jewish people. This volume, by Cecil Roth, is one of the best. It is divided into six parts, of which two are devoted to the ancient period (1600 B.C.–425 A.D.), one to the Middle Ages, and three to modern times. In treating the Jewish people in antiquity, Roth takes full account of the findings of modern biblical criticism, but argues that "the memory of a whole people," even when it may be contradicted by scholarship, has a "subjective historicity" with a truth of its own.

• Saggs, H. W. F., **The Greatness That Was Babylon:** *A Survey of the Ancient Civilization of the Tigris-Euphrates Valley* [1962] (New York: Praeger. $13.00; Mentor paperback, $2.25). Written for high schoolers, college freshmen, and the general reader, this is a comprehensive history of Babylonia and Assyria illustrated with more than sixty pages of plates. The opening chapters, devoted to political history, are a bit heavy-going in places, but the nine chapters that follow on Mesopotamian society and culture have a broader appeal. With the help of liberal excerpts from the primary sources, Saggs describes social life, government, trade, religion, literature, science, and art. There is also a summary of what Western civilization owes to the Babylonian achievement. For a study of the incredible city of Babylon and its rediscovery by modern archeologists, read James Wellard's **Babylon** (New York: Saturday Review, 1972. $6.95).

Wilson, John A., **The Burden of Egypt:** *An Interpretation of Ancient Egyptian Culture* (Chicago: U. of Chicago Press,

1951. $7.50; as **The Culture of Ancient Egypt,** Phoenix paperback, $2.45). This is probably the most valuable short book in the English language on ancient Egypt. Wilson has integrated social, cultural, economic, and political history in a series of brilliant interpretative essays on the major periods of ancient Egyptian history from its prehistoric beginnings to the post-imperial age of the early first millennium B.C. He looks on the ancient Egyptians as a basically optimistic people who owed their view of life and their theory of divine kingship to their favorable geographical position in the ancient world. "Egypt was the land which was cut off from major contacts and thus enjoyed a happy sense of security and special election. Her destiny was exceptional because divine providence had set her apart—distinctly apart—from her neighbors." Wilson also tends, as many other scholars have done, to idealize the early dynasties and regret the conservatism and decadence of the later ones. The Old Kingdom of the first dynasties was "the period of Egypt's rich and abundant youth," a time of scientific curiosity, political inventiveness, and pride of craftsmanship far beyond anything achieved in her neurotic old age.

2. Greece and Rome

Africa, Thomas W., **Rome of the Caesars** (New York: John Wiley, 1965. Paperback, $3.95). Africa constructs a wry, unsentimental picture of imperial Rome in the first two centuries of the Christian era. His approach is biographical. After an introductory chapter on the city itself, he sketches the lives of eleven men who figured, each in his own very different way, in the political and intellectual history of the early Empire. Among others, we meet a court politician (Sejanus), a client prince (Herod Agrippa), a Christian missionary (Paul), a Stoic philosopher (Seneca), an Asian wizard (Apollonius of Tyana), and two emperors (Hadrian and Marcus Aurelius). The author quotes liberally from the primary sources, believing that "the Roman world is best seen through Roman eyes."

Bultmann, Rudolf, **Primitive Christianity in Its Contemporary Setting** [1949](New York: Meridian paperback, $3.95). The greatest of twentieth-century New Testament scholars examines the historical background of early Christianity and provides its gospel with an existentialist interpretation. Bultmann's own theological position takes work to understand, despite the clarity and forcefulness of his prose, but this book is chiefly valuable for its penetrating discussion of the intellectual and spiritual sources of Christian thought in the Hellenistic world. Bultmann explores, in order, the impact of the Old Testament, of later Judaism, of classical Greek culture, and of the philosophies and religious cults of the Hellenistic age. Primitive Christianity, he concedes, was "full of tendencies and contradictions . . . the outcome of syncretism." At the same time it possessed a unity of its own and a new, unique doctrine of human existence characterized by "radical openness for the future."

Deissmann, Adolf, **Paul:** *A Study in Social and Religious History* [1911] (New York: Harper, 1957. Reprinted by Gloucester, Mass.: Smith, $5.50). This is a passionate defense of St. Paul against the common charge that he substituted for the gospel of Jesus a theology of redemption hopelessly contaminated with pagan philosophy and superstition. Deissmann traces Paul's life in its Jewish, Greek, and Roman setting, and expounds his religious world-view. "The Christ-centred Christianity of Paul," he concludes, "is the necessary form in which alone the Master's revelation could be assimilated by mankind, and which alone was capable of fashioning a perennial religion for the people." Another excellent German study of Paul's life and thought is Günther Bornkamm, **Paul** (New York: Harper, 1971. $7.50). Bornkamm makes good use of recent research on the problem of the authorship of the letters ascribed to Paul in the New Testament. He also supplies a much fuller account of Paul's career as a missionary.

Gibbon, Edward, **The Decline and Fall of the Roman Empire** [1776–88] (3 vols., New York: Modern Library, 1932. $4.95 each; 3 vols., Pocket Books paperback, $2.95 the set). Gibbon's classic history of the later Roman Empire and the Middle Ages to 1453 qualifies as perhaps the best known and most influential historical work of the modern era. It is marked by scrupulous scholarship, literary artistry of the highest rank, and the typical prejudices of the eighteenth-century Enlightenment. Gibbon regarded Rome's fall as "the triumph of barbarism and religion," the conquest of a benevolent, if despotic, state by dark forces that he could not fully understand, much less approve. He had little sympathy for the medieval aftermath of Rome in the West or for the later Byzantine empire in the East, but fortunately most of the *Decline and Fall* is devoted to a detailed study of the centuries that he found least distasteful, from the death of Marcus Aurelius in 180 A.D. to that of Heraclius in 641. Although his view of Christianity as one of the chief causes of Rome's fall took courage to hold in an age when any attack on the Christian religion was still punishable by law, it has few supporters today. Nevertheless, this is a work of prodigious learning and eloquence; no one should attempt to teach the history of late antiquity who has not read it.

• Hamilton, Edith, **The Greek Way to Western Civilization** (New York: Norton, 1930. $6.95; paperback, $1.75). "Five hundred years before Christ in a little town on the far western border of the settled and civilized world," writes Edith Hamilton, "a strange new power was at work. . . . Athens had entered upon her brief and magnificent flowering of genius." *The Greek Way* is a lyrical study of art, literature, and religion in fifth-century Athens. The greatness of Athenian culture, according to Hamilton, derived from its achievement of an uncanny balance between the demands of mind and spirit, the generalizing tendencies of mind and the individualizing tendencies of spirit, a balance unknown elsewhere in the ancient world and rarely struck by Western man in medieval or modern times. This is a deservedly popular book, enriched with many delightful excerpts from Greek literature, but it suffers from the author's inability to empathize with any ancient culture except the classical Greek. The results are at best ingenuous, at worst sentimental and even a little dishonest.

●   Kitto, H. D. F., **The Greeks** (Chicago: Aldine, 1951. $7.50; Penguin paperback, $1.25). Kitto is a professor of Greek literature who loves his subject, and the ancient Greeks themselves, with a quiet passion. His twelve chapters are a happy blend of history, geography, political science, literary criticism, and history of philosophy and religion, treating most of the significant aspects of preclassical and classical Greek life with humor and good sense. But do not be deceived by Kitto's informal style. Although his manner is casual, his reverence for the Greek way of life runs deep, and at times he overstates his case. The ancient Greeks, he writes on his first page, discovered "a totally new conception" of the meaning of life and "showed for the first time what the human mind was for." The author also shares Aristotle's judgment of the superiority of the *polis* to all other state-forms in the ancient world. Two other exceptionally good surveys of Greek civilization by British scholars are C. M. Bowra, **The Greek Experience** [1957] (New York: Praeger. $10.00; Mentor paperback, $1.25), and M. I. Finley, **The Ancient Greeks:** *An Introduction to Their Life and Thought* (New York: Viking, 1963. $5.00; Compass paperback, $1.45).

     MacMullen, Ramsay, **Constantine** (New York: Dial, 1969. $7.95; Torchbooks paperback, $2.95). The best of several recent biographies of the first Christian emperor. MacMullen writes in a clear, simple style that goes straight to the point, not unlike the emperor he portrays. He argues that Constantine was an early and ardent convert to Christianity who had little interest in its theology and less in its moral implications, but who perceived at once its practical value. "He aimed at the prosperity of his reign and realm through ensuring to God acceptable worship, and by prosperity he evidently had in mind quite material well-being: an end to civil war, security along the borders, plentiful crops for a plentiful population—in short, peace and its products."

•   Payne, Robert, **Ancient Rome** [1966] (New York: American Heritage, 1970. $6.95; paperback, $2.95). Originally published as *The Horizon Book of Ancient Rome,* this is a colorful treatment of Rome by an old master of popular history. With the help of many plates, lively prose, a large stock of anecdotes, and a genius for condensation, Payne offers a narrative history of Roman civilization in the classical age that is easy on both eye and mind.

    Rostovtzeff, M. I., **Greece** [1924] (New York: Oxford U.P., 1963. $10.00; paperback, $2.75). **Rome** [1924] (New York: Oxford U.P., 1960. $10.00; paperback, $2.50). Hailed as "the only fundamental reinterpretation" of the collapse of ancient civilization since Gibbon, the work of the émigré Russian historian M. I. Rostovtzeff is here presented in an abridged edition of one of his best known books, *A History of the Ancient World* (first published in English in two volumes in 1926–27). Rostovtzeff's forte was social and economic history, but in these volumes he offers what is basically a political narrative. He concludes that the decline and fall of both Greece and Rome can be explained by the aristocratic nature of ancient civilization, which alienated the masses and led finally to military dictatorship by rough-hewn soldier-demagogues who pulverized the ruling elites of the old aristocratic order and helped to destroy its culture through their sheer inability to understand it. Rostovtzeff's thinking was powerfully influenced by the fate of his own native Russia, where the transition from aristocratic decadence to democratic despotism had occurred in less than a decade.

Syme, Ronald, **The Roman Revolution** (New York: Oxford U.P., 1939. $15.25; paperback, $5.75). Few books in the field of ancient history have excited so much critical acclaim as Sir Ronald Syme's *The Roman Revolution*. Through a careful study of the factional struggles within the ruling class of the Roman Republic in the first century B.C., he shows that the establishment of the principate under Augustus was not the triumph of an ideology but the usurpation of power by a cold-hearted factional boss, who broke the ascendancy of the Roman nobility and brought political stability to the empire through fraud and bloodshed.

Syme's Rome has no heroes, republican or imperial. Yet on balance he seems to prefer the dictator Augustus to the rapacious oligarchs of the late Republic. With all his faults, Augustus did more than seize power; he created a whole new form of government for Rome, Italy, and the empire, a system "firm, well-articulated and flexible . . . neither exclusive nor immobile," that survived its founder by many centuries. But whatever one may think of Syme's assessment of Augustus, his greatest achievement as a scholar is his collective biography of the Roman aristocracy, based on a detailed exploration of family history.

Tarn, W. W., **Hellenistic Civilization** [1927] (3rd ed., New York: St. Martin's, 1952. $8.50; Meridian paperback, $3.45). **Alexander the Great** [1948] (Boston: Beacon paperback, $2.45). The "Hellenistic" age is the period between the career of Alexander the Great and the final emergence of Rome as the political and, in some respects, cultural center of Mediterranean antiquity. During these three centuries the Greeks first conquered the Western world and then lost their own independence; at the same time, they "Hellenized" most of the peoples with whom they came in contact, including the Egyptians and the Romans. Greek culture, with certain inevitable modifications, became Western culture. The emphasis properly falls, in Tarn's *Hellenistic Civilization,* not on the rather dreary and inconclusive political history of the period, but on the diffusion of Greek culture, on trade and exploration, literature and learning, science and art, philosophy and religion.

Alexander the Great is Tarn's biography of the Macedonian emperor, a delightfully concise and provocative account of his life which concludes with the controversial thesis that Alexander is not only the historical prototype of the imperial warlord but a creative and visionary thinker who dreamed of world brotherhood and world peace. "He was one of the supreme fertilizing forces of history."

Watson, G. R., **The Roman Soldier** (Ithaca, N.Y.: Cornell U.P., 1969. $7.50). No one had more to do with the *Pax Romana* than the Roman soldier. In this short, readable, and fully documented monograph, the author follows a typical recruit through his career, from enlistment to retirement, and assesses "the impact of the serving soldier and veteran upon the society in which he found himself." We learn how soldiers were recruited and trained, their opportunities for promotion, conditions of service, and religious and marital life. Since this is social and institutional, rather than military, history, Watson does not discuss warfare as such. He finds that most Roman G.I.'s were "content with their lot. The direction of social mobility for the soldier was normally upward."

Zimmern, Alfred, **The Greek Commonwealth:** *Politics and Economics in Fifth-Century Athens* [1911] (5th ed., New York: Oxford U. P., 1931. Paperback, $2.75). Occasionally a work of scholarship remains the leading authority in its field through several generations. There is still no better general study of the politics and economic life of Athens in its golden age than this book, now more than sixty years old, by the English political scientist Sir Alfred Zimmern. His approach is topical, rather than chronological, but within each topic he also indicates the course of historical development, with generous attention to the pre-classical beginnings of Athenian life. Four chapters discuss the geographical background, eight are devoted to politics and government, seventeen to economics, and a final chapter treats the Peloponnesian War, which brought the fifth century and, with it, much of the greatness of Athens to a tragic end.

chapter four | Traditional Asia

With the possible exception of Israel, none of the societies of the ancient West exists today, or has existed for hundreds of years. Christianity, Islam, and modern secularism long ago absorbed and transformed them all. It is quite otherwise with the classical civilizations of east and middle Asia, which did not even begin to disintegrate until the nineteenth century. In some countries they are still far from extinct, despite headlong change in recent decades. Unlike the Egypt of the Pharaohs or the Rome of the Caesars, such great societies as Hindu India and Confucian China did not fall during the ancient or medieval periods in Western history. They have "fallen," if at all, only under extreme pressures emanating from the Western world in our own century.

It therefore makes sense to explore traditional Asian history in a single chapter that ranges from the prehistoric period all the way to 1945. I have subdivided the chapter into three parts —"East Asia," "South and Central Asia," and "The Islamic Middle East." "East Asia" is defined as China, Japan, and Korea. "South and Central Asia" embraces the Indian subcontinent, Southeast Asia from Burma to the Philippines, and Central Asia from Turkistan to Mongolia. In the former, the parent civilization was China; in most of the latter, India. Japan, Korea, and Central and Southeast Asia did not develop civilized societies until the early centuries of the Christian era, and then only under direct Chinese or Indian influence.

The Islamic Middle East stands in a class by itself. From a contemporary perspective, the Islamic world, which stretches from Morocco to Indonesia, is only another example of a traditional and chiefly Asian culture now rapidly changing in the face of the Western challenge. But from the point of view of the Western peoples until recent times, Islam was a second-generation civilization, rooted in Judeo-Christian and classical values, and the chief rival of medieval and early modern Christendom in the struggle to inherit the Roman empire. In one sense, therefore, the Islamic Middle East belongs in our next chapter, on medieval and early modern Europe. Or perhaps it should have a chapter of its own.

But each of the three major cultures included in the present chapter is a human universe with its own life-style, mental climate, distinctive institutions, and unique pattern of historical evolution. Each has interacted vigorously with the others, and each has met its most dangerous challenge in the last two centuries, with the rise to world power of modern secularized Western civilization. The acid test of any course in world history is its success or failure in coping with these alien universes, so unlike our own, and yet so incredibly rich in fundamental human experience at all levels.

1. East Asia

Benedict, Ruth, **The Chrysanthemum and the Sword:** *Patterns of Japanese Culture* (Boston: Houghton, 1946. $6.95; Meridian paperback, $3.45). During the second World War, the anthropologist Ruth Benedict made a careful study of Japanese culture for the American government. She could not visit the country she was studying, and was in no sense a Japanese expert, but she received much help in her work from interviews with overseas Japanese. Her training in anthropology enabled her to construct a perceptive working model of manners and mores in traditional Japan. She discovered a minutely stratified society with a rigorous code of behavior that kept life at "high tension." As one might expect of an anthropologist, her chapters are analytical rather than historical, with titles such as "Taking One's Proper Station," "Clearing One's Name," and "Self-Discipline."

• Cottrell, Leonard, **The Tiger of Ch'in:** *The Dramatic Emergence of China as a Nation* (New York: Holt, 1962. $5.00). Better known for his books on Egyptology, Leonard Cottrell turns his attention here to the early history of China, with emphasis on the men most responsible for the cultural and political unification of the Chinese people: Confucius, Shih Huang-ti (the "Tiger of Ch'in"), and Liu Pang (founder of the Han Dynasty). The prose is vigorous, the scholarship adequate, although this is not a book for specialists.

Creel, H. G., **The Birth of China:** *A Study of the Formative Period of Chinese Civilization* [1937] (New York: Ungar. $9.75; paperback, $2.75). One of the major archeological discoveries of this century occurred in the district of Anyang in north China. Here scholars working from 1928 to 1937 unearthed the ruins of the capital city of China's first historic culture, the Shang. This Bronze Age culture flourished in the second half of the second millennium B.C. before giving way to the so-called Chcu Dynasty, which in turn survived until the third century B.C., when all of China was unified by the royal house of Ch'in. Creel's book is an account for the general reader of the archeological discoveries at Anyang, together with a survey of what is known of Shang culture and the China of the early Chou period. He based his work exclusively on Chinese sources.

• Creel, H. G., **Confucius:** *The Man and the Myth* (New

York: John Day, 1949. As **Confucius and the Chinese Way,** Torchbooks paperback, $2.75). Beyond dispute, Confucius (in Chinese, K'ung-fu-tzu) is the greatest figure in Chinese history; perhaps even in world history, since no other philosopher or religious teacher has exerted so profound an influence on the whole structure of his civilization. In this critical reinterpretation of Confucius, H. G. Creel attempts to show that the Master's teachings were deliberately perverted by apologists for imperial autocracy long after his death. The real Confucius was neither a propagandist for absolute monarchy nor a defender of the feudal status quo but a "forerunner of democracy," a liberal humanist who "advocated and helped to bring about such sweeping social and political reforms that he must be counted among the great revolutionaries." Creel argues that his thought also played an important part in the Western Enlightenment and in shaping the republic founded by Sun Yat-sen. For an excellent nontechnical survey of the history of Chinese philosophy that includes several chapters on Confucius and Confucianism, see the same author's

● **Chinese Thought from Confucius to Mao Tse-tung** [1953] (New York: Mentor paperback, $0.95).

● Gernet, Jacques, **Daily Life in China in the Thirteenth Century** [1959] (New York: Macmillan, 1962. $4.95. As **Daily Life in China on the Eve of the Mongol Invasion, 1250–1276,** Stanford U. P. paperback, $2.95). The largest and richest city in the world in the middle of the thirteenth century was probably Hangchow, now one of southern China's smaller urban centers, but at that time the thriving capital of the Sung Dynasty with a population that reached one millon. Drawing chiefly on Chinese documents of the period, and on the memoirs of Marco Polo, who knew the city well, Gernet recreates everyday life in the Sung capital in the generation before it fell to the Mongols in 1276. We see the city, its people, their clothing and cuisine, their lives from birth to death, their religious observances, and their

amusements, arts, and literature. Broader in scope and also at-
● tractively written is Michael Loewe, **Everyday Life in Early
Imperial China During the Han Period 202 B.C.–A.D. 220**
(New York: Putnam, 1968. $5.00; Perennial paperback, $1.25).

●   Goodrich, L. Carrington, **A Short History of the Chinese People** [1943] (New York: Torchbooks paperback, $1.75).
For many years this has been the best brief account of Chinese
history, by a distinguished China specialist at Columbia University. Well under 300 pages in length, it nevertheless manages to
cover the whole span of Chinese history from Neolithic times and
contains many bits of unusual information that throw new light
on the topics treated. For longer but often less insightful textbooks of Chinese history, see K. S. Latourette's **The Chinese:**
Their History and Culture [1934] (4th ed., New York: Macmillan, 1964. $12.50) and Dun J. Li, **The Ageless Chinese** [1965]
(2nd ed., New York: Scribner, 1972. $15.00; paperback, $5.95).

●   Grousset, René, **The Rise and Splendour of the Chinese
Empire** [1943] (Berkeley: U. of California Press, 1953. Paperback, $2.45). This is a colorful, absorbing, narrative history of
China centered on government and court life in the earlier imperial dynasties, from the Ch'in to the collapse of Mongol rule
in 1368. Grousset also gives some attention to culture and socioeconomic problems. He resorts frequently to analogies with Western history. Shih Huang-ti, for example, was the "Chinese
Caesar," who set up a "Pax Sinica" in East Asia. There is no
documentation, little analysis, few striking hypotheses, but *The
Rise and Splendour of the Chinese Empire* makes good bedtime
reading.

  Hall, John Whitney, **Japan from Prehistory to Modern
Times** (New York: Delacorte, 1970. $9.95; Dell paperback,
$2.95). Although Japan did not give rise to a classic civilization
of her own, writes John Whitney Hall, "It has been the particular
destiny of the Japanese that they have lived within two contrast-

ing great traditions (Chinese and Western), and it has been through their genius that, while accommodating to both, they have achieved some stature and distinction in each." Japan has undergone Sinicization and Westernization without losing her identity or her capacity for self-determination. Thanks to her geographical position, the pattern of Japanese history has been predominantly linear rather than cyclical: a pattern of steady cumulative growth, undisturbed by foreign aggression despite the powerful influence of foreign cultures. Most of Hall's book deals with the earlier periods in the Japanese experience. Another recent one-volume history of Japan is Mikiso Hane, **Japan:** *A Historical Survey* (New York: Scribner, 1972. $15.00; paperback, $6.95).

• Hart, Henry H., **Marco Polo, Venetian Adventurer** [1942] (Norman, Okla.: U. of Oklahoma Press, 1967. $6.95). Marco Polo spent most of the last quarter of the thirteenth century in the service of the greatest ruler of his era, Kublai Khan, emperor of the Mongols and founder of the Yüan Dynasty in China. Hart's biography makes an invaluable companion volume to Polo's memoirs, although only part of it concerns his hero's travels and work in China. Other chapters discuss Polo's boyhood and his life in Italy after he returned to Europe in 1295. To this intrepid—but also charming and industrious—Venetian, Westerners have long owed their most intimate glimpse of life in imperial China.

Lattimore, Owen, **Inner Asian Frontiers of China** (New York: American Geographical Society, 1940). Lattimore addresses himself to one of the most important themes in Chinese history: the interaction of agricultural China with the peoples of the steppe and the forest on her frontiers. He suggests that on both sides political and economic life followed a four-stage cyclical pattern. The Chinese had their dynastic cycles, the nomads their tribal cycles. From the inner Asian "reservoir," barbarian invaders often broke into the empire, but no permanent integration of a society based on intensive agriculture could occur with a fundamentally pastoral society. At the end of each cycle, both sides returned to their original way of life, and the cycles started over again.

Michael, Franz, **The Taiping Rebellion:** *History* (Seattle: U. of Washington Press, 1966. $8.50; paperback, $3.95). By any standard of measurement, the Taiping "rebellion" of 1850–64 was one of the most extraordinary and fateful civil wars in world history. Sixteen provinces of China were involved. Six hundred cities were devastated. Millions of lives were lost. The Taipings, a fanatic and puritanical religious sect that blended Chinese and Christian ideas in equal proportion, nearly overthrew the Ch'ing Dynasty; it is as if the American Civil War had been fought between the Union and Joseph Smith's Mormon Saints. Michael sees the Taiping movement as a precursor of modern totalitarianism, although he can find no direct historical connection between it and the later revolutions in Chinese history. The rebellion "signalled the beginning of the end of Confucian China."

Reischauer, Edwin O., John K. Fairbank, and Albert M. Craig, **A History of East Asian Civilization** (2 vols., Boston: Houghton, 1960–64. $12.50 and $13.50). An eminent team of Harvard scholars has written this well received two-volume textbook of the history of China, Japan, and Korea. It is a beautifully produced set, with more than 150 photographic plates and 1,700 pages of text and maps. The first volume, subtitled *The Great Tradition,* surveys East Asia to "the eve of modernization": China and Korea to the early nineteenth century, Japan to the end of the Tokugawa period in 1867. In the second volume, *The Modern Transformation,* the authors carry their narrative down to the 1960's, with additional chapters on the "peripheral areas" of Southeast Asia, the East Indies, and the Philippines. The set is not marked by boldness of conception or unusual felicity of style, but it supplies a sound, lucid, well-balanced exposition of East Asian history. Both volumes are based on a lecture course inaugurated by the senior authors, Reischauer and Fairbank, in 1939.

●   Reischauer, Edwin O., **Japan:** *The Story of a Nation* [1947] (4th ed., New York: Knopf, 1970. $6.95; paperback, $4.95). Reischauer's new book is a rewritten version of his *Japan, Past and Present,* first published in 1947. Earlier periods are covered briefly, but the emphasis falls on the twentieth-century history of Japan. Reischauer is obviously quite sympathetic both to the Japanese people and to the policies followed by the United States in Japan during the Truman-MacArthur years. He predicts that Japan may become the world's most important country before the end of this century, an industrial superpower and the mediator between East and West in world affairs. See also, by the same author, **The United States and Japan** [1950] (3rd ed., Cambridge, Mass.: Harvard U. P., 1965. $8.00; Compass paperback, $2.25), especially Parts II and III.

    Sansom, Sir George B., **A History of Japan** (3 vols., Stanford: Stanford U. P., 1958–63. $10.00, $10.00, and $8.50; paperback, $4.95, $4.95, and $3.45). A British diplomat from 1904 to 1947, Sir George Sansom spent most of his career in Japan, where he acquired not only a mastery of the diplomatist's skills but also became the English-speaking world's leading scholar of premodern Japanese history. The three volumes and 1,200 pages of his *History of Japan* were written after he retired from the diplomatic service and accepted a professorship at Columbia University. As examples both of the historian's literary art and of professional scholarship based firmly on primary sources, they are unequaled in the whole field of East Asian studies. The first volume follows Japanese history to 1334, the second to 1615, and the third to 1867, the end of the Tokugawa shogunate. This is now the standard authority on traditional Japan in Western languages. For a less detailed account by the same author, originally published before the war, see **Japan: A Short Cultural History** [1931] (rev. ed., New York: Appleton, 1962. $8.95).

●   Sharman, Lyon, **Sun Yat-sen:** *His Life and Its Meaning, A Critical Biography* [1934] (Stanford: Stanford U. P., 1968. $8.75; paperback, $2.95). The Chinese contemporary and counterpart of Gandhi, Sun Yat-sen was elevated after his death in 1925 into what Sharman calls a "lacquered image," a national divinity, very much like Mao Tse-tung today (except that China's current idol is alive). She took as her task in this pioneering biographical study the rediscovery of the historical figure who was already disappearing from view under layers of hastily contrived political mythology in the Nationalist China of the 1930's. Her study of Dr. Sun is affectionate, but severely honest. Since she could not read Chinese, it is based entirely on sources in Western languages. She concludes that her subject was not a truly great leader but typified the somewhat superficial impact of Western ideas on late imperial China, an impact "characterized by over-confidence and under-thinking."

     Tan, Chester C., **The Boxer Catastrophe** [1955] (New York: Octagon. $8.50; Norton paperback, $2.25). A Chinese scholar tells the complex story of the rebellion against foreign influence waged by the "Boxers" in 1899–1900, which was crushed in the end by a fantastic polyglot army drawn from eight different countries, including the United States. Tan traces the Boxers to their origins in secret societies. For younger readers,
● there is Burt Hirschfeld's **Fifty-Five Days of Terror:** *The Story of the Boxer Rebellion* (New York: Messner, 1964. $3.95).

     Wright, Arthur F., **Buddhism in Chinese History** (Stanford: Stanford U. P., 1959. $4.75; paperback, $1.95). The role of Buddhism in Chinese history is sometimes compared to that of

Christianity in Western history. Both were evangelistic faiths of personal salvation developed by historic messiahs from a rich background of religious tradition. Both enjoyed their greatest success on foreign soil.

In this short study, originally a series of six lectures delivered at the University of Chicago, the Yale historian Arthur F. Wright follows Buddhism in Chinese history from its almost unnoticed arrival in the first and second centuries A.D. to its period of greatest influence and power, between the fourth and eighth centuries, to its eventual assimilation into the mainstream of Chinese culture, much weakened as an independent force. He shows that China may have done more to Buddhism than Buddhism did to China; it could not have gained a foothold at all in the alien ground of Confucian China had the Chinese not experienced temporary disillusionment with their traditional way of life as a result of the economic, political, and socio-cultural collapse of the civilization of the Han dynasty in the third century. *Buddhism in Chinese History* is a clear and penetrating study of a major theme in the history of China by a distinguished scholar.

2. South and Central Asia

Allchin, Bridget and Raymond, **The Birth of Indian Civilization:** *India and Pakistan Before 500* B.C. (Baltimore: Penguin, 1968. Paperback, $2.25). Two British archeologists survey the current state of knowledge about the prehistoric cultures on the Indian subcontinent, from the Early Stone Age to the Aryan invasions and the "beginnings of history." The first seven chapters review the sequence of cultures in more or less chronological order; the last four study patterns of settlement, economic life, crafts, art, and religion in the whole region throughout the prehistoric period. Relatively little space is devoted to the most spectacular archeological "find" on the subcontinent, the Indus civilization of the third and second millennia B.C., but so much basic research has been done recently in other areas that the briefness of the Allchins' treatment of this remarkable culture is no doubt justified. This is a sound, workmanlike volume, fitted out with many excellent plates and drawings.

●   Basham, A. L., **The Wonder That Was India:** *A Survey of the Culture of the Indian Sub-Continent Before the Coming of the Muslims* [1954] (3rd ed., New York: Taplinger, 1968. $13.50; Evergreen paperback, $4.95). If you wish to read only one book on ancient India, this is no doubt the one to select. Despite the somewhat bumptious title, it is a rich, sophisticated, humane, and profusely illustrated general account of ancient Indian life by a University of London scholar who knows his subject well. Nearly 600 pages long, it has two "historical" and six "topical" chapters, examining in depth ancient Indian politics, society, everyday life, religion, the arts, and language and literature. An epilogue sums up "the Heritage of India." Basham manages to show a respectful sympathy for traditional Indian culture without descending into sentimentality.

    Grousset, René, **The Empire of the Steppes:** *A History of Central Asia* [1939] (New Brunswick, N.J.: Rutgers U. P., 1970. $17.50). For more than a thousand years, the warrior nomads of inner Asia periodically conquered the great civilizations on their borders. Many of the central figures are familiar names: Attila, Genghis and Kublai Khan, Tamerlane. *The Empire of the Steppes,* by the French orientalist René Grousset, enables us to understand the social and military dynamics of this important period in Asian history. Grousset attributes the victories of the nomad to the harshness of his land and the superiority of his military technique, based on his skills as a huntsman. "The mounted archer of the steppe reigned over Eurasia for thirteen centuries because he was the spontaneous creation of the soil itself: the offspring of hunger and want." Only the development

of artillery in the sixteenth century gave his intended victims enough superiority in fire-power to defeat him. This large, beautifully written, and carefully researched volume is one of Grousset's finest accomplishments. A handsome sequel is his
● biography of Genghis Khan, **Conqueror of the World** [1944] (Compass paperback, $2.45).

Hall, D. G. E., **A History of South-East Asia** [1955] (3rd ed., New York: St. Martin's, 1968. $13.50; paperback, $6.95). "Southeast Asia" is a term that originated during the second World War and has now become so familiar that we may wonder how we ever managed without it. This now standard textbook by D. G. E. Hall of the University of London defines Southeast Asia as Burma, Thailand, Indochina, Malaya, and the East Indian archipelago. Perhaps unwisely, Hall omits the Philippines. Until the coming of the Europeans, the major cultural influence throughout the region (except in Vietnam) was Indian, an influence that Hall finds comparable to the Greek influence in western Europe, all the more since the Indians played no political role in Southeast Asia, just as the Greeks never conquered Europe. At the same time, the countries of Southeast Asia "are not mere cultural appendages of India or China but have their own strongly-marked individuality."

● Humphreys, Christmas, **Buddhism** (Baltimore: Penguin, 1951. Paperback, $1.65). Christmas Humphreys is a British lawyer and judge who founded the Buddhist Society of London in 1924 and has written several books expounding Buddhist thought to Western readers. A lay Buddhist, who takes what might be called an ecumenical approach to the various "denominations" of Buddhism, Humphreys sees value in all of them. Together, they constitute "the most comprehensive and profound school of spiritual achievement known to history," a serenely optimistic faith whose purpose "is to attain Enlightenment, for oneself and all creation." After a biography of the

Buddha and an account of the early growth and diffusion of the Buddhist faith, the author supplies chapters on Theravada, Mahayana, Zen, and Tibetan Buddhism. Although he is not a professional scholar, and knows no Oriental languages, he has been in close contact with leading Buddhist thinkers throughout the world for many years, and his *Buddhism* is a valuable introduction to the history and doctrines of a great world religion.

Hutton, J. H., **Caste in India:** *Its Nature, Functions, and Origins* [1947] (4th ed., New York: Oxford U. P., 1963. $2.75). A distinguished Cambridge anthropologist attempts to explain what is probably the most difficult institution in traditional Indian society for Westerners to understand, much less accept. Hutton sees the Indian caste system as peculiar to the subcontinent, although he recognizes that somewhat analogous institutions have existed elsewhere, as, for example, in ancient Egypt, in Burma, and in Japan. After a detailed study of the structure, sanctions, and functions of caste, he advances a multi-causal theory to explain its historical origins. He lays special emphasis on the geographical position of India, a vast cul-de-sac that has "trapped" many different peoples at many different levels of socioeconomic development, requiring the elaboration of an exceptionally complex social structure. Also significant, in his view, is the indigenous pre-Hindu culture of Southeast Asia, and in particular its web of "beliefs in *mana,* taboo and magic," on which many later social distinctions may have been based.

● Moffat, Abbot Low, **Mongkut, the King of Siam** (Ithaca, N.Y.: Cornell U.P., 1961. $7.50; paperback, $1.95). No Asian monarch in history is so well known to Americans as Mongkut, who ruled Siam (Thailand) from 1851 to 1868. In books, plays, films, and now television, Mongkut has been represented as "half devil, half child," a semibarbarous despot with a curious weakness for Western science who dramatizes the problems faced by traditional Asia in her modern confrontation with Western culture. Unfortunately, the famous account of Mongkut given by his children's British governess, Anna Leonowens, on which all the stage productions are based, is a thoroughly unreliable brew of reminiscences, gossip, and stories about other Asian rulers falsely attributed to Mongkut. Mrs. Leonowens was more a novelist than a historian.

This modest biography by Abbot Low Moffat tries to set the record straight, with the help of the king's own writings. Mongkut emerges as a devout, tolerant, conscientious, enlightened monarch. For seventeen years he "steered his country through the conflicting pressures and territorial ambitions of France and England and set the course that preserved the independence of his country." The author includes an appendix on "Anna as Historian."

•   Nehru, Jawaharlal, **The Discovery of India** (New York: John Day, 1946. Reprinted by New York: Asia Society, $7.50; abridged and edited by Robert I. Crane, Garden City, N.Y.: Doubleday, 1959, Anchor paperback, $1.95). Like *Glimpses of World History,* reviewed in our first chapter, *The Discovery of India* was written while Nehru was a political prisoner of the British. In this book, he supplies an interpretative history of India from the earliest times to the second World War. Conceding that British rule in India had its benefits, he deplored the way in which British imperialism hampered the political development of the Indian people and deprived them of their just share in modern Indian prosperity. He also attacked the movement among Muslim Indians for a separate Pakistani state as a return to "feudalism." In the words of an American reviewer, *The Discovery of India* is "a most moving love story of a man's affection for his native land."

•   Payne, Robert, **The Life and Death of Mahatma Gandhi** (New York: Dutton, 1969). Biographies of Gandhi are legion, but they are rarely the work of specialists in Indian history. Payne is a virtuoso biographer with a gift for well researched story-telling; his book on Gandhi is predictably strong in "human interest," weak as a study of modern Indian history. It begins with Gandhi's birth in 1869, closes with an account of the execution in 1949 of the Hindu fanatics who plotted his assassination, and remains narrowly focused on its hero throughout its more than 700 pages. The prose is colorful, and at times purplish, as some of the chapter headings suggest: "An Enchanted Childhood," "The Storm Breaks," "A Fast unto Death," "The Fire and the Fury." Another interesting book is Erik H. Erikson's **Gandhi's Truth** (New York: Norton, 1969. $10.00; paperback, $2.95), which detects "a correspondence in method and a convergence in human values" between Freudian psychoanalysis and Gandhian militant nonviolence.

Spear, Percival, **India:** *A Modern History* [1961] (rev. ed., Ann Arbor, Mich.: U. of Michigan Press, 1972. $10.00). Although the author's announced purpose in this book "is to portray the transformation of India under the impact of the West into a modern nation state," he offers an interpretative overview of the whole range of Indian history from ancient times. His analyses are penetrating; his narrative style is brilliant; and he has full command of his sources. On the difficult question of whether British rule helped or hindered the growth of present-day India, Spear argues persuasively that the British influence was, on the whole, a good thing. He also notes the importance of the Mughal period, which helped pave the way for modernization under the British Raj.

For another recent history of India, see **A History of India** (2 vols., Baltimore: Penguin, 1965–66. Paperback, $1.75 and $1.45). The first volume, by Romila Thapar, surveys traditional India and the second, by Spear, covers the period since the founding of the Mughal Empire in 1526.

Zimmer, Heinrich, **Philosophies of India** [1951] (Princeton: Princeton U.P. $12.50; paperback, $3.95). Many scholars convert their lecture notes into books. Zimmer's *Philosophies of India* is based on notes for lectures delivered at Columbia University that his colleague Joseph Campbell arranged in the form of a book after his untimely death in 1943. This sometimes makes for unsatisfactory results, especially in the section on "the worldly philosophies" of politics, ethics, and sex, but Zimmer's unfinished book far surpasses the average scholar's most polished production. His *forte* is empathetic understanding of the more esoteric aspects of Indian thought: "specialized learning directed to the attainment of a higher state of being." Such learning, Zimmer points out, is not academic. It aims not at objective knowledge but at self-transformation, and has always been considered a secret doctrine, requiring long years of training and accessible only to a few extraordinary individuals. The Indian philosopher is more like a champion athlete than a scholar.

The miracle of Zimmer's book, and presumably of his lectures at Columbia also, is that he manages to introduce Western readers to this esoteric teaching in a delightfully personal, easy-going, almost conversational style fortified with many helpful excerpts from Indian literature. Reading Zimmer may not convert you into an Indian philosopher, but it enables any reasonably intelligent Western mind to gain a clear view of the thrust and purpose of this decidedly non-Western mode of thought. Readers of *Philosophies of India* may also wish to tackle another of Zimmer's books, **Myths and Symbols in Indian Art and Civilization** [1946] (Princeton: Princeton U.P. $7.50; paperback, $2.95).

3. The Islamic Middle East

Fisher, Sydney N., **The Middle East:** *A History* [1959] (2nd ed., New York: Knopf, 1968. $10.50). Written chiefly for the college student, this well constructed textbook provides a general survey of Middle Eastern history since Mohammed. Its four main parts discuss the rise and spread of Islam, the Ottoman Empire to 1815, European imperialism in the Middle East from the French Revolution to 1914, and the contemporary Middle East, with emphasis on developments since 1945. The approach is more or less conventionally political, but within its limits this is an excellent treatment of Middle Eastern history. For a much briefer review of the same area during the same years, a good book to consult is George E. Kirk, **A Short History of the Middle East** [1948] (7th ed., New York: Praeger, 1964. $7.50; paperback, $3.50).

●   Hitti, Philip K., **The Arabs:** *A Short History* [1943] (5th ed., New York: St. Martin's, 1969. $5.95; Gateway paperback, $0.95). Philip K. Hitti is a Syrian-American scholar who has perhaps done more than any other single writer in this country to promote an understanding of the history of the peoples of the Middle East. Many of his books come in two sizes: the complete work in six or seven hundred pages, and a shorter edition for the general reading public. Such is the case with his **History of the Arabs,** originally published in 1937, and now in its tenth edition (New York: St. Martin's, 1970. $12.50; paperback, $8.95). The abridgement, *The Arabs: A Short History,* covers the same ground as the larger volume in less than a quarter of its length. Anyone with a special interest in the Arabs will want to consult the unabridged book, but this shorter work offers a convenient survey of Arab history, both political and socio-cultural. Hitti's presentation is clear, unobtrusively sympathetic, and well organized. But readers should be warned that he gives only very brief attention to the Arab countries in the modern world: his emphasis falls heavily on what, from the Western point of view, is the "medieval" period in Arab history, from the rise of Islam to the European Renaissance.

●   Hitti, Philip K., **Makers of Arab History** (New York: St.

Martin's, 1968. $6.95; Torchbooks paperback, $2.75). This is something like a companion volume to Hitti's *History of the Arabs*. Here he exchanges the narrative approach for the biographical, with sketches of the life and times of thirteen eminent figures in medieval Arab history. In the first part of the book, Hitti gives us seven religious and political leaders. Mohammed is hailed as "the ablest Arab in history . . . the triple initiator of religion, nation and state." Others studied include Omar, "founder of the Moslem empire" and Saladin, "hero of the anti-Crusades." One name conspicuously among the missing is Harun al-Rashid, who figured in many tales in the "Arabian Nights," but Hitti does devote a chapter to his equally significant son, the caliph al-Mamun, who made Baghdad "an intellectual capital of the world." In a second section reserved for leaders of Arab thought, Hitti discusses such major Arab intellectuals as al-Ghazzali, Avicenna, Averroes, and Ibn Khaldun.

Holt, P. M., et al., eds., **The Cambridge History of Islam** (2 vols., New York: Cambridge U. P., 1970. $19.50 each). The traditional interpenetration of faith and state in Islamic countries, the kinship felt by all members of the "house of Islam" throughout the world, and the historic world empires founded by Muslim rulers make it possible to transcend geographical categories and write a universal history of Islamic life. *The Cambridge History of Islam* performs this difficult task in a work of collective scholarship by an international team of scholars in two volumes and almost 1,800 pages. Volume One deals with the "central Islamic lands" of the Near East in four large sections, from Mohammed to recent times. Volume Two surveys the history of the "further Islamic lands" of the Indian subcontinent, Southeast Asia, Africa, and Europe, and also offers thirteen topical chapters on Islamic society and civilization.

Kinross, Lord, **Atatürk:** *A Biography of Mustafa Kemal, Father of Modern Turkey* (New York: Morrow, 1965. $10.00).

Each November 10 at 9:05 A.M., everyone in Turkey stops whatever he is doing to pay silent homage to the memory of Mustafa Kemal Atatürk, who died on that day in 1938 after fifteen years as first president of the Turkish republic. Kinross's biography is a colorful popular account of Atatürk's life, based on extensive research in the primary sources. Its three parts, of about equal length, study his career during the last years of the Ottoman empire, in the war of independence, and as president of the republic. Kinross concedes that Atatürk was a dictator, but a dictator who pursued "liberal ends." "He differed from the dictators of his age in two significant respects: his foreign policy was based not on expansion but on retraction of frontiers; his home policy on the foundation of a political system which could survive his own time."

Lewis, Bernard, **The Arabs in History** [1950] (4th ed., New York: Hutchinson, 1966. $4.50; Torchbooks paperback, $1.95). Lewis has written a brilliant interpretative study of Arab history from pre-Islamic times. After an introduction that tackles the difficult question of the meaning of the word "Arab," he discusses Arabia before the coming of Islam, the career of Mohammed, the establishment of the Arab world empire, the appearance of schisms in Islam, the Arab states in Europe, medieval Islamic civilization, the decline of Arab world power, and the Western impact in modern Arab history. Throughout, Lewis shows a keen awareness of the importance of socioeconomic factors in Middle Eastern history. The establishment of the Abbasid caliphate in Baghdad, for example, is viewed not merely as a change of dynasties but as a revolution comparable to the French or Russian revolutions in European history. It marked the replacement of the old Arab warrior aristocracy with a new social order based in Mesopotamia on a peace-time economy of agriculture and commerce.

Lewis, Bernard, **The Emergence of Modern Turkey**

[1961] (2nd ed., New York: Oxford U. P., 1968. Paperback, $3.95). This definitive study of the "Turkish Revolution" proposes that to understand how the essentially medieval Ottoman empire was transformed into the modern, secular, national Turkish republic, one must begin not with the spectacular events of the 1920's but with the eighteenth century. The Turkish Revolution, writes Lewis, "has been going on for nearly two centuries. It began when a series of defeats at the hands of once-despised enemies forced the Turks, for the sake of survival, to adopt European weapons, to invite European advisers, and thus, however reluctantly, to admit all the new ideas and institutions that underlie the modern state and army." The first part of Lewis's book reviews in chronological sequence "the Stages of Emergence," to 1950. In the second part, "Aspects of Change," he discusses Turkish nationalism, the theory and practice of government, the interaction of Islam and secularism, and the socioeconomic order of modern Turkey. *The Emergence of Modern Turkey* is the best work available in English on modern Turkish history, but for a convenient shorter study see Roderic H. Davison, **Turkey** (Englewood Cliffs, N.J.: Prentice, 1968. $5.95; Spectrum paperback, $1.95).

●   Merriman, R. B., **Suleiman the Magnificent, 1520–1566** [1944] (New York: Cooper. $6.00). For nearly half a century (1520–1566) the ruler of the Ottoman Empire was the sultan Suleiman I, known to Westerners as Suleiman the Magnificent and to Turks as Suleiman the Lawgiver. It was Suleiman who added Rhodes, Belgrade, and most of Hungary to Turkish rule, laid unsuccessful siege to Vienna in 1529, conducted full-scale naval war in the Mediterranean against the European powers, and terrified most of Christendom. At home, he ruled with wisdom and moderation, and patronized the arts. This biography by the popular Harvard historian Roger Bigelow Merriman is not a classic, but it was written with boyish enthusiasm and does justice at least to the military exploits of its subject. "The longer one studies him," Merriman says of Suleiman, "the greater he seems to be." For Harold Lamb followers, there is also Lamb's

- **Suleiman the Magnificent:** *Sultan of the East* (Garden City, N.Y.: Doubleday, 1951).

- Payne, Robert, **The Holy Sword:** *The Story of Islam from Mohammed to the Present* [1959] (New York: Collier paperback, $0.95). The versatile Robert Payne sweeps through the whole history of Islam, but his interest centers on the earlier periods. He covers the last seven centuries in two chapters. "Today we see only the husk of Islam," he writes, "shorn of its ancient grandeur." Nevertheless, its one-time grandeur is beyond dispute, and "all that was best in Islam came, not from the sword, but from the contemplation of God's peace." This is a well paced popular introduction to Islamic history.

Von Grunebaum, Gustave E., **Medieval Islam:** *A Study in Cultural Orientation* [1946] (2nd ed., Chicago: U. of Chicago Press, 1953. $6.75; Phoenix paperback, $3.45). Von Grunebaum is an imaginative specialist in Islamic studies with a penchant for sweeping generalizations. *Medieval Islam* is an essay in intellectual history. "It proposes to outline the cultural orientation of the Muslim Middle Ages, with Eastern Islam as the center of attention. It attempts to characterize the medieval Muslim's view of himself and his peculiarly defined universe, the fundamental intellectual and emotional attitudes that governed his works, and the mood in which he lived his life."

Watt, W. Montgomery, with Pierre Cachia, **A History of Islamic Spain** (Chicago: Aldine, 1965. $6.00). For nearly eight centuries after the Moorish conquest in 711–16, Spain was better known as al-Andalus, an Islamic country closely linked to the centers of medieval Islamic civilization in North Africa and the Near East. In this history of Moorish Spain, Watt contends that al-Andalus owed nothing to pre-conquest Visigothic Spain, but was in every sense an organic part of the Islamic world, making great contributions to its art, literature, and philosophy. The text is enriched with magnificent photographs of Moorish architecture (including the Alhambra in Granada) by Wim Swaan.

Watt, W. Montgomery, **Muhammad:** *Prophet and Statesman* (New York: Oxford U. P., 1961. $9.75; paperback, $1.85). This is an abridgement of Watt's two-volume biography of Mohammed (Arabic scholars prefer "Muhammad"), originally published in 1953 and 1956: **Muhammad at Mecca** and **Muhammad at Medina** (New York: Oxford U.P. $9.50 and $8.00). The special value of Watt's approach is not his insight into the personality of Mohammed, where he has little new to offer, but his profound understanding of the relationship between the social context in which Mohammed lived and the success of his prophetic mission. The author shows that Islam was precisely the kind of religious faith needed by the rising commercial towns of the Arab world in the seventh century A.D. Pagan Arab culture, with its nomadic ethic of personal courage and tribal loyalty, had little relevance for urban merchants. Mohammed's faith supplied an ethic better suited to the needs of urban society and a wider loyalty, to God and his prophet, the bearer of God's word. Mohammed was also—in Watt's judgment—an inventive statesman and social reformer, who translated his vision of righteousness into a new political order that made possible the unification of the Arab people for the first time in their history. For a more intimate study of the Arab prophet, by a psychologist of religion, consult Tor Andrae, **Mohammed:** *The Man and His Faith* [1930] (New York: Harper. Torchbooks paperback, $1.95).

chapter
five | Traditional
Europe

Until after the collapse of the Roman empire in the West, a true
European civilization did not exist. Although the ancient Greeks
and Romans had originated on the European mainland, both
peoples established themselves on the Afro-Asian as well as
European shores of the Mediterranean. But as Christianity
yielded to Islam in Africa and Asia, new societies emerged that
belonged almost wholly to Europe: the Greek Christian civilization of her southeastern quarter and the Roman Christian civilization of her western half. Greek Orthodox Christendom eventually widened to include Russia; Roman Catholic Christendom
pushed northeastward to civilize Scandinavia, Poland, and
Hungary.

From the beginning, then, Europe consisted of two rival
Christian societies. The present-day division of the continent into
"Communist" and "bourgeois" camps continues in a new way
the old competition. Moscow has inherited the imperial claims of
Constantinople. The countries of the Common Market have
succeeded Roman Christendom.

Our task in this chapter is to review books in the field of
"medieval" and "early modern" European history. This is an un-

usually difficult undertaking, not only because an immense slice of history is involved, but also because far more English-language scholarship is available on Europe than on any other field in world history. Most of the important books cannot even be mentioned; there are too many.

But we shall do what we can. Reviewed here are works in the history of the Middle Ages, the Renaissance, the Reformation, and the seventeenth and eighteenth centuries to 1789, a period of more than thirteen hundred years during which Europe grew steadily from a disorganized mass of wandering tribes to a constellation of kingdoms collectively more powerful than any other civilized society in the world. Most of the titles will stress the evolution of the major Western states, such as Italy, Spain, France, England, and the Germanic states of central Europe, but we must also save some space for Orthodox Christendom, especially the Byzantine Empire and Russia.

I have deliberately included the "medieval" and "early modern" periods in the same chapter because I see no sharp break between them. Europe's progress from the fall of Rome to the fall of the *ancien régime* in France followed an even course. The Middle Ages were not—as we have long realized—a period of stagnation, but of rapid recovery and growth. The early modern centuries, from the Italian Renaissance to Frederick the Great, were not—as we are beginning to see—a period of unprecedented vigor but of organic continuity with trends established long before. Only after 1789 does the pace of change accelerate drastically, catapulting all mankind into the modern world. Before 1789 traditional Christian Europe was the latest example in a long series of traditional civilizations, comparable in wealth, power, and culture to many others in world history. It was a great civilization, but not an authentically "modern" one—not global, not industrial, not democratic. On the other hand, it was perhaps the only traditional civilization capable of fathering the modern world. One of our most important responsibilities as historians is to discover the seeds of modernity in the inner life of traditional Europe.

1. The Middle Ages

• Adams, Henry, **Mont-Saint-Michel and Chartres** [1904] (Boston: Houghton. $6.00; Sentry paperback, $2.65; Anchor paperback, $1.95). After seventy years, this remains one of the most sensitive and beautiful books ever written about the culture of the High Middle Ages, by one of the founders of Amercan historiography and a grandson of John Quincy Adams. Mont-Saint-Michel is the island monastery on the coast of Normandy, Chartres the great cathedral near Paris, both rebuilt in Gothic style early in the thirteenth century. But Adams did much more than write a tourist's guide to architectural masterpieces: he sought to lay bare the medieval "soul." Although some professional medievalists would not agree, his book furnishes a good introduction to the study of the art and thought of medieval Western Christendom.

• Barraclough, Geoffrey, **The Medieval Papacy** (New York: Harcourt, 1968. $5.95; paperback, $3.75). The central institution in Western European medieval life was the Church, which had firmly established itself long before the fall of Rome. But the Roman papacy, as Geoffrey Barraclough writes, was "in its most essential ways a creation of medieval Europe." Not until the sixth century did the term "pope" come to be reserved for the bishops of Rome; not until the eighth did the bishops of Rome secure their independence from Constantinople; not until the pontificate of Gregory VII (1073–85) did the papacy emerge as an imperial power within the Church and in western Christendom as a whole. This beautifully illustrated history of the papacy to the middle of the fifteenth century is by a distinguished medievalist who summarizes here the results of nearly forty years of study.

Barraclough, Geoffrey, **The Origins of Modern Germany** [1946] (2nd ed., New York: Barnes, 1948. $5.50; Capricorn paperback, $2.95). As a national state in modern times, Germany goes back no further than 1871. During the Middle Ages it existed in another, much weaker form, as the Holy Roman Empire founded by Otto of Saxony in the tenth century. Barraclough's book, written during the second World War when its author was on active service in the Royal Air Force, attempts to trace the historical origins of "the German problem."

He sees the basic source of that problem in medieval and early modern Germany's historic failure to build effective institutions of national government that could give her people a tradition of unity. German history, he writes, "is a story of discontinuity, of development cut short, of incompleteness and retardation." The villain in the piece was "princely particularism," which sabotaged the medieval German monarchy and continued to frustrate German aspirations toward unity in early modern times. "By stifling the development of the middle classes and accumulating social and economic privileges in the hands of the few, it prevented the peaceful evolution of German life into democratic forms capable of expressing the will of the German people."

Billington, James H., **The Icon and the Axe:** *An Interpretive History of Russian Culture* (New York: Knopf, 1966. $15.00; Vintage paperback, $3.45). The key word in the title of this book is "interpretive." Billington makes no claim "of offering an encyclopedic inventory of the Russian heritage." Rather he has written a highly personal interpretation of medieval and modern Russian culture that seeks "to locate and trace symbols that have played a unique role for the Russian imagination." The icon and the axe, "traditionally hung together on the wall of the peasant hut in the wooded Russian north," serve as starting points, suggesting both the visionary and the earthy aspects of Russian culture. Billington may be faulted for his lack of attention to political and economic forces, but this is a powerful book.

Bloch, Marc, **Feudal Society** [1939–40] (Chicago: U. of Chicago Press, 1961. $12.50; 2 vols., Phoenix paperback, $1.95 each). This is the last book of the French medievalist Marc Bloch, whose career was cut short by the Gestapo in 1944 after he had joined the French Resistance. Bloch was more of a social scientist than a historian. He set out in this book to analyze the structure of feudalism in terms of its responsiveness to concrete human needs and in terms of the whole environment of medieval life, including the climate of ideas in which the institutions of feudalism flourished. Its eight parts discuss the significance of the last barbarian invasions for the origins of feudalism, the material and intellectual background, ties of kinship and vassalage, the manorial system, the classes of medieval society, feudalism and political organization, and the place of European feudalism in world history. This is a long book, but its clear and vigorous style makes it accessible to anyone with a serious interest in medieval European life.

Cantor, Norman F., **Medieval History:** *The Life and Death of a Civilization* [1963] (2nd ed., New York: Macmillan, 1969. $11.50). Like many other scholars of the younger generation, Cantor is well aware of the limitations of political history. His interests run more to social and intellectual history, but he has avoided the temptation to pursue them in isolation from the rest of life. In this college textbook, detailed discussions of thought, religion, and culture are "fully integrated with the analysis of political, economic, and social change in order to attempt a genuine synthesis of the pattern of medieval civilization." Chronologically, Cantor's emphasis falls on the earlier Middle Ages. Ten chapters explore the sources of medievalism in antiquity and the growth of Europe to the beginning of the eleventh century; ten chapters deal with the High Middle Ages; and two study the period of breakdown and dissolution after 1350.

Huizinga, Johan, **The Waning of the Middle Ages** [1919]

(New York: St. Martin's. $9.50; Anchor paperback, $2.50). The Black Death, economic depression, and cultural decline mark the fourteenth and early fifteenth centuries in most of northern Europe. Frenchmen, Germans, Lowlanders, and Englishmen found themselves living in a bewildering, unhappy age, an age that seemed to reverse the progressive tendencies of earlier times. To peer into the mind and heart of this troubled period was the project of the Dutch historian Johan Huizinga in *The Waning of the Middle Ages,* a pioneering essay in social psychology that has wielded a wide influence since it was first published more than half a century ago. Huizinga's sources were the works of art and literature of the age, in the Netherlands and northern France. Wherever he turned, whether to "a chronicle, a poem, a sermon, a legal document even, the same impression of immense sadness is produced. . . . A general feeling of impending calamity hangs over all. Perpetual danger prevails everywhere." Both in depth of insight and in richness of style, few works in the field of cultural history bear comparison with *The Waning of the Middle Ages.*

• Kelly, Amy, **Eleanor of Aquitaine and the Four Kings** (Cambridge, Mass.: Harvard U. P., 1950. $10.00; paperback, $2.75). Every once in a while, a scholar writes a biography that outshines almost any historical novel, both in readability and in the power to bring a period vibrantly alive. Amy Kelly's *Eleanor of Aquitaine* is one of these, a finely wrought study of the life and times of a remarkable woman of the twelfth century. Queen first of Louis VII of France and then of Henry II of England, she was also the mother of King Richard Lion-Heart and King John. Through her inheritance of the duchy of Aquitaine (capital city, Bordeaux), this important part of France belonged to the English crown for four hundred years.

Ostrogorsky, George, **History of the Byzantine State** [1940] (rev. ed., New Brunswick, N.J.: Rutgers U. P., 1969. $15.00). For more than eleven hundred years, a "Roman" empire flourished in Asia Minor and the southeastern quarter of Europe. In the eyes of its eighty-eight emperors and empresses, it inherited the full power and majesty of imperial Rome. But throughout most of its history the Byzantine state was in fact only an expanded version of ancient Greece, just as the "Holy Roman Empire" in the West was only a medieval precursor of modern Germany.

In this standard political history of Byzantium, George Ostrogorsky follows its ups and downs from the founding of Constantinople in the fourth century A.D. to the fall of the city to the Turks in 1453. He hails the empire as "the instrument by means of which Graeco-Roman antiquity survived through the ages," and from which (during the Renaissance) it "passed on to the peoples of western Europe who were now ready to receive it."

● Painter, Sidney, **Mediaeval Society** (Ithaca, N.Y.: Cornell U. P., 1951. Paperback, $1.95). For the beginning student, there is no better introduction to the everyday world of the High Middle Ages than Painter's *Mediaeval Society*. Barely one hundred pages in length, it views England, France, and western Germany from the tenth to the thirteenth centuries in three essays explaining the feudal system, the organization of agriculture, and the development of towns and commerce. A short concluding section summarizes the changes that took place in medieval life during the three centuries covered.

Pirenne, Henri, **Economic and Social History of Medieval Europe** [1933] (New York: Harcourt. Harvest paperback, $1.65). For many years professor of history at the University of Ghent in Belgium, Pirenne first made his mark as a historian of his own country. But his reputation today rests chiefly on the work of his last years, when he turned to far-reaching interpretative syntheses of the economic history of Europe during the Middle Ages. Here he studies the revival of commerce in the early medieval period, the rise of the cities, and the progress of international trade to the fourteenth and fifteenth centuries. He argues that trade created cities, instead of the other way around, a view that works much better for the Lowlands, which Pirenne knew especially well, than for other parts of Europe. In any event, Pirenne assigned the credit for making medieval Europe to her merchants, the solid burghers of towns like his own Ghent. Only two chapters are devoted to agriculture.

Pirenne, Henri, **Mohammed and Charlemagne** [1937] (New York: Barnes. $5.00; paperback, $1.95). Just as there is more than one "Einstein theory," there is more than one "Pirenne thesis," but when medievalists speak of the Pirenne thesis, they are usually referring to the argument of this book, which the great Belgian scholar finished in 1935, the year of his death. Working from the perspectives of economic history, Pirenne maintained that the Roman world did not come to an end in the fifth century with the seizure of the Western empire by Germanic barbarians. Social and economic life continued much as before. Only in the seventh and eighth centuries after the spread of Islam had deprived Christendom of its control of the Mediterranean did a radically new society begin to develop in northwestern Europe that deserves to be called "medieval." In short, antiquity ended not with the fall of Rome but with the rise of Islam.

Runciman, Sir Steven, **Byzantine Civilisation** [1933] (New York: St. Martin's. $8.50; Meridian paperback, $3.45). This is a study of "the qualities that characterized Byzantine history throughout its length." After two chapters on the founding of Constantinople and the political history of the empire from 330 to 1453, Runciman discusses Byzantine law, administration, religion, the military, the diplomatic service, commerce, town and country life, education, literature, art, and relations with "the neighboring world." The empire had so many enemies, and hovered so often on the brink of destruction, that its typical citizen "inevitably sought comfort in ultra-mundane things, in union with God and the hope of eternal life. He knew existence to be sad. The simple laughter and happiness of the pagans was lost."

Runciman, Sir Steven, **A History of the Crusades** (3 vols., New York: Cambridge U. P., 1951–54. $17.50 each; vol. 2 only, Torchbooks paperback, $3.45). Anyone seriously interested in the Crusades will find these volumes by Sir Steven Runciman an indispensable work of reference. In spite of their length, they will also please the general reader. Runciman is a master of the grand style in history, a fine stylist as well as a fine scholar. The first volume deals with the First Crusade and the foundation of the Latin Kingdom of Jerusalem, the second with the history of the kingdom to the capture of Jerusalem by Saladin in 1187. Volume Three surveys the crusades of the late twelfth and thirteenth centuries, together with the declining years of the Latin Kingdom to the fall of its last stronghold, Acre, in 1291. Runciman explains not only the motives and deeds of the European Crusaders but also "the circumstances in the East that gave to the Crusaders their opportunity and shaped their progress and their withdrawal. Our glance must move from the Atlantic to Mongolia."

In his summing-up, he characterizes even the successes of the Crusades as the triumph of "faith without wisdom." For all their glamor, the Crusades were "a tragic and destructive episode" in world history, "a long act of intolerance in the name of God, which is the sin against the Holy Ghost."

Trevor-Roper, Hugh, **The Rise of Christian Europe** (New York: Harcourt, 1965. $5.50; paperback, $3.25). Trevor-Roper is a feisty but always interesting Oxford historian, who refuses to "stay put" in the fields he knows best. A specialist in seventeenth-century England, he roams in this little book through the Middle Ages, daring the professional medievalists to criticize him as they will. He centers his attention on several major problems: the causes of Rome's fall, the Pirenne thesis, Europe's precipitous decline in the late Middle Ages, and the reasons for her resurgence after 1450. Trevor-Roper does an outstanding job of integrating the history of medieval Western Europe with that of Byzantium, Islam, and Central and East Asia. Included are 124 handsome maps and illustrations, many in color.

White, Lynn, Jr., **Medieval Technology and Social Change** (New York: Oxford, 1962. $9.00; Galaxy paperback, $1.75). "The role which technological development plays in human affairs," says Lynn White, Jr., "has been neglected." But not in the three essays that make up this unusual book. White shows how the invention of the stirrup contributed to the development of the feudal warrior aristocracy in the early Middle Ages; how heavy ploughs, horse-collars, and the three-field system revolutionized society; and how European man had already made the transition to a machine technology by the close of the Middle Ages. White concludes that in technological development Europe far surpassed the rest of the world as early as the fifteenth century. This is a fascinating book, although some readers will prefer to skip the footnotes which are as long as the text itself.

● Wilson, David M., **The Vikings and Their Origins:** *Scandinavia in the First Millennium* (New York: McGraw, 1970. $5.95; paperback, $2.95). The last major barbarian terror in western Europe occurred during the eighth to the tenth centuries when her coasts were often raided and sometimes settled by fierce sea-borne pagan warriors from Denmark and Norway. Others, from Sweden, penetrated and conquered much of ancient Russia. David M. Wilson's book discusses the origins of the Vikings, their exploits in Europe, and their life at home. The text is brief, but thoroughly reliable, and there are 110 illustrations.

2. Renaissance and Reformation

● Bainton, Roland H., **The Reformation of the Sixteenth Century** (Boston: Beacon, 1952. Paperback, $1.95). The Protestant Reformation is often closely identified with the rise of capitalism, the Renaissance voyages of discovery, the growth of the centralized national state, and the arrival of the "modern" age. But Roland H. Bainton points out in this fine history of the Reformation that it "was not derived from any of these other movements. . . . The Reformation was above all else a revival of religion." If it shattered the unity of medieval Christendom, it may also be regarded as "the renewer of Christendom. . . . The Reformation made religion and even confessionalism a paramount issue in politics for another century and a half." In other words—to stretch Bainton's point just a little—the Reformation belongs more to the medieval than to the modern world. It looked backward, seeking to purify a church allegedly corrupted by the blasphemous innovations of "popery."

After three opening chapters on Luther's faith and career, Bainton runs the rest of the gamut of Protestant rebellion from the Zwinglians, Anabaptists, and Calvinists to such "free spirits" as Sebastian Franck and Michael Servetus. He also tells the story of the religious wars of the sixteenth century, the establishment of the Church of England, the struggle for religious liberty, and the impact of the Reformation on political and economic life and thought. The text is superbly illustrated with sixteenth-century woodcuts.

Bindoff, S. T., **Tudor England** (Baltimore: Penguin, 1950. Paperback, $1.65). Bosworth Field, Cardinal Wolsey, Henry VIII, Bloody Mary, Elizabeth I, Mary Queen of Scots, Sir Walter Raleigh, the Spanish Armada, Shakespeare and Spenser—all belong to the glorious history of the dynasty that ruled England from 1485 to 1603. It is difficult sometimes to imagine how all of them (and a great deal more) fitted into so short a span of years. This witty, reliable, and humane history of Tudor England captures the romance of the sixteenth century with no sacrifice of scholarly values.

Burckhardt, Jacob, **The Civilization of the Renaissance**

in Italy [1860] (2 vols., Torchbooks paperback, $1.95 and $1.45). For more than a century, Burckhardt's great book has been the point of departure for all serious students of the Italian Renaissance. The Swiss historian first published it in 1860, offering an interpretation of the Renaissance in Italy as an era of tough-minded paganism, in which professional politicians ruthlessly schemed for power and enlisted the services of writers and artists to add luster to their regimes. The nature of his thesis led Burckhardt to make a penetrating inquiry into the relationship between politics and culture. His book has also done much to develop the now common view of the Italian Renaissance as the first age of modernity, the first decisive breakaway of European civilization from the values of the Middle Ages. I think Burckhardt was wrong, but this is a book that should not be missed.

Chabod, Federico, **Machiavelli and the Renaissance** (Cambridge, Mass.: Harvard U. P., 1958. Torchbooks paperback, $2.75). In these seminal essays, a historian of the University of Rome undertakes to "present Machiavelli, the author of *The Prince,* as the expression, almost the synthesis of Italian life throughout the fourteenth and fifteenth centuries; to see reflected and clarified in his thought . . . the age-long process of development which leads from the downfall of the old Communal freedom to the triumph of the princely, the absolute State." More than half of Chabod's book studies *The Prince,* Machiavelli's best known work. There are also two essays on his "method and style" and on "the concept of the Renaissance." Machiavelli emerges from Chabod's analysis as a tragic and often contradictory thinker, but also as an architect of the modern spirit and a passionate Italian patriot.

Dickens, A. G. **The Counter Reformation** (New York: Harcourt, 1969. $6.95; paperback, $3.50). Catholics understandably resent the term "Counter Reformation," since it suggests that the reformation of the Roman Catholic Church in the sixteenth and early seventeenth centuries represented a reaction against, and a response to, the Protestant Reformation, rather than something that would have occurred anyway, with or without Protestantism to spur it on. An outstanding British Reformation specialist, Dickens holds that the Catholic Reformation was both things at the same time: an answer to the Protestant challenge and a movement already under way before Luther's rebellion. In two hundred pages tastefully fortified with more than 100 illustrations, Dickens introduces us to the medieval sources of the Catholic revival, the rise of the Jesuits, the Council of Trent, the role of the papacy, and the religious culture of the Counter Reformation: its devotional life, art, thought, and charitable enterprises. This is a volume in the *History of European Civilization Library,* to which A. G. Dickens has also contributed **Reformation and Society in Sixteenth-Century Europe** (New York: Harcourt, 1966. $5.50; paperback, $3.25).

• Elliott, J. H., **Imperial Spain:** *1469–1716* (New York: St. Martin's, 1964. $7.95; Mentor paperback, $0.95). The European great powers have a way of rising and falling with almost indecent suddenness. Between 1870 and 1945 Germany twice "rose" and "fell" again. Throughout most of the nineteenth century, the ascendant power was Britain. France dominated the European world from the age of Louis XIV to the Battle of Waterloo.

In this strongly recommended book by the Cambridge historian J. H. Elliott we follow the rise and fall of a country that emerged from obscurity to play the leading role in the sixteenth century: imperial Spain. In a hundred years Spain built the world's largest empire, acquired enormous wealth, championed the Catholic Reformation, and enriched Western civilization with the art of Cervantes, Lope de Vega, and El Greco. But by the latter part of the seventeenth century, Spain had faded again to mediocrity, and Elliott lays most of the blame on the reluctance of her ruling classes to keep up with the times. "Seventeenth-century Castile," he writes, "had become the victim of its own history, desperately attempting to re-enact the imperial glories of an earlier age. . . . At a time when the face of Europe was altering more rapidly than ever before, the country that had once been its leading power proved to be lacking the essential ingredient for survival—the willingness to change."

Erikson, Erik H., **Young Man Luther:** *A Study in Psychoanalysis and History* (New York: Norton, 1958. $6.50; paperback, $1.75). Historians, even those who write biographies, seldom attempt to psychoanalyze their subjects. They are unfamiliar with psychoanalytic techniques, and most of their subjects, in any event, are unavailable for the analyst's couch. But things are changing. Erikson's *Young Man Luther* is an exciting breakthrough in the infant science of "psycho-history."

Erikson centers on Luther's early manhood, on his relations with his father and his "identity crisis"—a concept developed by Erikson in his work as a practicing psychoanalyst. This book has done much to stimulate the use of psychoanalytic techniques by professional historians, and no one can fail to learn from it. The standard modern biography of Luther stressing his faith and thought is Roland H. Bainton, **Here I Stand:** *A Life of Martin Luther* (Nashville: Abingdon, 1950. $6.95; Mentor paperback, $1.25).

Mattingly, Garrett, **The Armada** (Boston: Houghton, 1959. $7.50; Sentry paperback, $2.65). It is not often that a historian can write a book about a romantically spectacular event, do the whole thing up in glorious language, and at the same time satisfy the most exacting demands of scholarship, viewing the event in its full historical perspective and dissolving the myths and legends that have encrusted it through the years. But this is Garrett Mattingly's achievement in *The Armada*. The first naval battle in history between ocean-going fleets is described in all its color and excitement. The political and diplomatic background is also traced, in considerable detail. We see the English, the Spanish, and indeed the whole European setting of this incredible battle. Mattingly shows that it did not bring Anglo-Spanish hostilities to a close or make England the mistress of the seas. But it did inflict a crushing defeat on Spanish aspirations to restore England and all of Europe to the Roman Catholic faith. After the humiliation of her "Invincible Armada," the boundlessly confident, crusading Spain of the sixteenth century existed no more.

• Neale, J. E., **Queen Elizabeth I** [1934] (New York: St. Martin's. $8.95; Anchor paperback, $2.50). Among the relatively few women who have held more than ceremonial power in world political history, Elizabeth I of England is one of the authentically towering figures. She ruled for forty-four years, walking a tightrope over a chasm boiling with religious and political problems that would have required all the skill of the greatest of male monarchs to cross in safety. Elizabeth rescued the Church of England, founded by her father Henry VIII, preserved England herself from Spanish conquest, and governed her kingdom with economy, wisdom, and broad popular support. One may dislike certain aspects of her personality, or credit some of her policies to brilliant councilors, or charge that she could not have coped with the rising gentry of the seventeenth century, but the fact remains that Elizabeth I was one of the greatest statesmen (statespersons?) of all time. Neale's biography is a narrative account of her life, written in clear, vivid prose by a first-rate scholar.

• Parry, J. H., **The Age of Reconnaissance** [1963] (New York: Praeger. $10.00; Mentor paperback, $1.50). To the Europe of the late fifteenth and sixteenth centuries goes credit for one remarkable accomplishment that sets her apart from any other traditional civilization in history: her seamanship. Western

European seamen were the first to bring all parts of the planet into consciousness of one another. Europe "discovered" the world, and in the process mankind began to discover itself. Parry's book tells "in outline the story of European geographical exploration, trade and settlement outside the bounds of Europe in the fifteenth, sixteenth and seventeenth centuries." It is also a careful examination of the backgrounds of discovery: the motives of those who sailed and the technical development of European seamanship that made such exploits possible for the first time. Here are all the early seafaring nations, the oceans they sailed, and the empires they founded abroad, skillfully presented in not much more than 300 pages. Parry is one of those rare scholars with the gift of seeing both trees and woods; to quote *The American Historical Review,* his book "is an achievement few could equal and fewer surpass."

Scarisbrick, J. J., **Henry VIII** (Berkeley: U. of California Press, 1968. $10.95; paperback, $3.85). J. J. Scarisbrick has written a big scholarly biography of England's greatest king, richly illustrated, with a substantial bibliography of printed and manuscript sources. In its pages, all the men and women around Henry shrivel more than a little. For Scarisbrick, Henry was the architect of the policies of his regime, a king of phenomenal intelligence and imagination, who "raised monarchy to near-idolatry" and became "the quintessence of Englishry and the focus of swelling national pride." The author deplores Henry's destruction of the monasteries and his foreign wars, but his reign "in many ways left a deeper mark on the mind, heart and face of England than did any event in English history between the coming of the Normans and the coming of the factory." Scarisbrick writes extremely well, and he knows his subject. This is a book to delight mind, heart, and eye. Still more recently, another important biography has appeared: Lacey Baldwin Smith's **Henry VIII:** *The Mask of Royalty* (Boston: Houghton, 1971. $8.95; Sentry paperback, $3.95). Smith stresses the heavy psychological burdens imposed by the Renaissance idea of divine right monarchy and Henry's nagging fears of his own inadequacy.

Schevill, Ferdinand, **The Medici** (New York: Harcourt, 1949. Torchbooks paperback, $1.95). This is a book about a family. Not an ordinary family, certainly! The Medici ruled Florence, the Athens of the Italian Renaissance, from the early fifteenth century to the early eighteenth. Bankers, statesmen, popes, mercenaries, patrons of high culture, they were a cross section of the ruling class of the Italy of their time. They provoked, and still provoke, fierce controversy.

Schevill tries to avoid the two extremes of enmity and partisanship in this collective biography of the Medici from their beginnings to the assassination of Alessandro de Medici in 1537. Medicean Florence in the fifteenth century "reveals the restless political striving and incomparable cultural burgeoning of one of the most creative communities within the whole compass of Western civilization."

Weber, Max, **The Protestant Ethic and the Spirit of Capitalism** [1904–06] (New York: Scribner, 1930. $5.95; paperback, $2.45). A German sociologist, Max Weber set forth in three articles published in 1904–06 one of the most hotly debated theses in modern historiography: the argument that the underlying "spirit" of capitalism was derived from the ethics of Protestantism, and specifically of Calvinism. The Calvinists advocated hard work in the everyday world; in Calvinism, the highest good was "the earning of more and more money, combined with the strict avoidance of all spontaneous enjoyment of life." Such an ethic, Weber held, inevitably did much to stimulate the rise of a capitalist economy in Europe, an economy of working and investing, as opposed to the more traditional economy which devalued labor and permitted the almost total consumption of its fruits.

The essays in this book have had a potent influence on

all our thinking about the Reformation. They have also come under devastating criticism. If only because capitalism originated among Catholics and Jews before the Reformation, and continued to flourish at least as well in non-Calvinist countries as in Calvinist ones throughout the sixteenth and seventeenth centuries, the Weber thesis is easily challenged. But anyone studying Reformation history should be familiar with it.

3. The Seventeenth and Eighteenth Centuries

Behrens, C. B. A., **The Ancien Régime** (New York: Harcourt, 1967. $5.50; paperback, $3.50). The *ancien régime* is the world that collapsed in the wake of the French Revolution: the world of absolute monarchy, aristocratic privilege, and ecclesiastical control of education and culture. C. B. A. Behrens analyzes the old order in France between 1748 and 1789 in its European setting. Only after 1748, she contends, did it begin encountering major problems that it could not solve and sophisticated opposition that it could not silence. Things went from bad to worse, inexorably. Serious attempts at reform were made, some of them quite far-reaching had they been carried through to completion, but the old order could not permit them to succeed, by the very nature of the forces that composed it. The bureaucratic despotism of old France dragged her along to her unavoidable death.

The Ancien Régime is an excellent introduction to eighteenth-century France, particularly valuable for its close study of the structure of society and the financial dilemmas of the royal government. But do not overlook Alexis de Tocqueville's nineteenth-century classic, which also found the Revolution inevitable, **The Old Regime and the French Revolution** [1856] (Garden City, N.Y.: Doubleday, Anchor paperback, $1.95), and Georges Lefebvre's **The Coming of the French Revolution** [1939] (Princeton: Princeton U.P., 1947. $6.50; paperback, $1.45).

Dorn, Walter L., **Competition for Empire:** *1740–1763*

(New York: Harper, 1940. $7.95; Torchbooks paperback, $2.75). The middle decades of the eighteenth century were the heyday of Frederick the Great, Voltaire, and William Pitt; the age of Dr. Johnson's *Dictionary,* the Lisbon Earthquake, and the Seven Years' War. Dorn captures it all with marvelous felicity. Here is the *ancien régime* at its highest point, the old prerevolutionary order of kings and lords and merchants in command of powerful states competing for imperial power in struggles that had lost the crusading character of the wars of the Reformation era and had not yet acquired the crusading character of the wars of modern democracy. The emphasis properly falls in Dorn's book on warfare and diplomacy; but in addition he furnishes excellent analyses of mid-century government, trade, and culture.

Friedrich, Carl J., **The Age of the Baroque:** *1610–1660* (New York: Harper, 1952. $7.95; Torchbooks paperback, $2.95). Friedrich's *The Age of the Baroque* is more than a competent outline of general European history from 1610 to 1660. It is a book with an imaginative thesis about the European state of mind in the seventeenth century. In a word, Friedrich believes that the whole era—and not just its art and architecture—should be characterized as "baroque." Seventeenth-century man preferred the baroque style in his art and architecture because the whole style of his life was baroque.

Of course everything hinges on how Friedrich defines his term. For him, the baroque spirit is one of restless striving, "an exaggerated belief in the power of man to think and to do as with heightened powers he confronts a mysterious, exciting world." Seventeenth-century man felt in his bones that nothing was too much for him, no design too grand, no goal too high. In cultural life, the baroque spirit expressed itself in the poetry of Milton and the statuary of Bernini. But Friedrich argues that it expressed itself no less clearly in the revolution in science and philosophy launched by Galileo and Descartes, in the political thought of

Hobbes, and, above all, in the emergence of the modern state. Such landmarks in the making of the modern state as the Thirty Years' War, the politics of Richelieu, and the revolution that began in England in 1642 were the work of men imbued with the same sense of power.

Gay, Peter, **The Enlightenment:** *An Interpretation* (2 vols., New York: Knopf, 1966–69. $10.00 each; vol. 1 only, Vintage paperback, $2.95). In two volumes totaling 1,260 pages Peter Gay has produced one of the most widely discussed studies of the Enlightenment to appear in many years. Do not be dismayed by its length. Gay knows how to write, for both an academic and a general reading public; the first volume of *The Enlightenment* was the winner of the 1967 National Book Award. Nor is he a mere compiler, heaping up names and dates. In the great debate over the modernity of the Enlightenment, he comes down hard on the side of the yea-sayers. For him the philosophers of the Enlightenment in eighteenth-century western Europe were just what many of them professed to be: radical enemies of the Christian heritage of Western civilization, neo-pagans who used the thought of pagan antiquity as a weapon against Christianity and then rejected the ancients in order to create their own modern science of man.

Gay has made a strong case for the revolutionary quality of eighteenth-century thought. The other side of the coin, the conservatism of the Enlightenment, is brought out with impish enthusiasm in Carl L. Becker's still thriving classic, **The Heavenly City of the Eighteenth Century Philosophers** (New Haven: Yale U. P., 1932. $5.75; paperback, $1.95).

Geyl, Pieter, **The Netherlands in the Seventeenth Century:** *1609–1715* [1934] (2 vols., New York: Barnes, 1961–64. $6.00 and $8.50). Pieter Geyl is a Dutch historian, and there are few better in any country. Here he studies the Netherlands in their greatest years, from the truce of 1609 that brought the northern provinces *de facto* independence from Spain to the death of their mighty adversary Louis XIV in 1715. The main theme of his first volume, and a major concern of the second, is the division of the Netherlands into two parts by the truce of 1609, confirmed in most particulars by the Treaty of Westphalia in 1648. The southern Dutch-speaking provinces of Flanders and Brabant remained under Spanish rule and developed along very different lines from those of the north. Geyl argues that when the Dutch war of independence broke out in 1581, no such differences had existed. A similar proportion of Catholics and Protestants could be found in north and south. But during and after the war, all was changed. The "violent disruption" of the "natural unity" of the Netherlands led in the north to "the triumph of Protestantism and the development of a particularist, North-Netherlandish patriotism, in Brabant and Flanders [to] the re-establishment of the Catholic Church in all her Counter-Reformation militancy." The results live on to the present day: the Netherlands is a predominantly Protestant country, and the old southern provinces are part of Catholic Belgium.

Equally choice is Geyl's **The Revolt of the Netherlands:** *1555–1609* [1931] (2nd ed., New York: Barnes, 1958. $6.25; paperback, $2.50).

Hill, Christopher, **The Century of Revolution:** *1603–1714* (New York: Nelson, 1961. Norton paperback, $2.25). "The years between 1603 and 1714," writes Christopher Hill, "were perhaps the most decisive in English history. . . . During the seventeenth century modern English society and a modern state began to take shape, and England's position in the world was transformed. This book tries to penetrate below the familiar events to grasp 'what happened'— to ordinary English men and women as well as to kings and queens or abstractions like 'society' and 'the state.' " Hill manages this very well, although readers whose recollection of kings and queens and wars is fuzzy may sometimes get lost along the way. He affirms that England during this vital century entered fully into the modern world, choosing parliamentary government instead of royal absolutism. But Hill also reminds us that the choice of freedom and self-government was a choice for men of property only. The life of the lower classes went on relatively unchanged, despite the premature efforts of the radical sects of the Civil War era to democratize English society. "Only very slowly and late have men come to understand that unless freedom is universal it is only extended privilege."

●   Koestler, Arthur, **The Sleepwalkers:** *A History of Man's Changing Vision of the Universe* [1959] (new ed., New York: Macmillan, 1968. $8.95; Universal paperback, $3.45). Author of *Darkness at Noon* and other novels, Arthur Koestler has also written an illuminating study of the Scientific Revolution of the sixteenth and seventeenth centuries. He finds that Copernicus, Brahe, Kepler, and Galileo were anything but "reasoning-machines on austere marble pedestals." Many of their ideas were old-fashioned, harking back to ancient science and mysticism. They arrived at some of their greatest theories accidentally, in a manner that "reminds one more of a sleepwalker's performance than an electronic brain's." Koestler's chapters on Johannes Kepler, his favorite "sleepwalker," are also separately available as

● **The Watershed:** *A Biography of Johannes Kepler* (Anchor paperback, $1.95). For a more orthodox treatment of the new science, see Herbert Butterfield, **The Origins of Modern Science, 1300–1800** [1949] (rev. ed., New York: Macmillan, 1957. Free Press paperback, $1.95).

●   Lewis, W. H., **The Splendid Century:** *Life in the France of Louis XIV* (New York: Sloane, 1954. Morrow paperback, $2.50). This is a social history of seventeenth-century France, by the younger brother of the novelist C. S. Lewis. It sparkles with all the rich and paradoxical life of France in the high noon of her history. Lewis opens with a pen portrait of Louis himself, to whom he accords "an exasperated and reluctant admiration. . . . It is easy to belittle Louis XIV, and yet it is no small achievement to have held the centre of the stage for over fifty years: and how many other kings have imposed their name upon a century?" Chapters follow on the great court at Versailles, the peasantry, the church, the army, the country gentry, the town, medicine, manners, life at sea, the education of girls, and the world of letters. Lewis saves his warmest praise for the literature of the age of Louis XIV. "It is the writers," men such as Corneille, Racine, and Molière, "not the soldiers, grandees and politicians, who gave the century its enduring place in the history of civilization; on their shoulders rests the claim of the Grand Siècle to the title of 'the splendid century'."

● Sumner, B. H., **Peter the Great and the Emergence of Russia** (New York: Macmillan, 1951. Collier paperback, $1.25). As Lenin transformed modern Russia into a socialist state, so "Peter the Great was decisive in the long process of transforming medieval Muscovy into modern Russia." This little book introduces us to one of history's most extraordinary people. He inherited a medieval throne, in a half-Asian country that took no part in the Renaissance or the Reformation. By the year of his death in 1725 at the age of fifty-two, he had brought Russia into full membership in the family of European nations. Sumner discusses the Tsar's wars on land and sea, his reform of civil government and the Russian Orthodox Church, his social and economic policies, and his place in history. As the man who almost single-handedly converted Russia into a great European power, and who initiated her political, military, and cultural Westernization, his place—Sumner feels—is secure.

Wedgwood, C. V., **The Thirty Years War** [1939] (New York: Fernhill. $15.00; Anchor paperback, $1.95). For nearly one hundred of the last 350 years, a general war has been in progress on the continent of Europe involving most of the Great Powers. The first of these general wars was the longest, the Thirty

Years' War of 1618–48, in which the principal contenders were Bohemia, the German states, Denmark, Sweden, Spain, the Netherlands, and France. C. V. Wedgwood's absorbing history of this tangled conflict, written in the aftermath of the first World War and on the eve of the second, reaches conclusions that would apply equally well to our twentieth-century struggles. The Thirty Years' War, she writes, was fought to little purpose and solved no problem. "Its effects, both immediate and indirect, were either negative or disastrous. Morally subversive, economically destructive, socially degrading, confused in its causes, devious in its course, futile in its result, it is the outstanding example in European history of meaningless conflict." The powers who fought, except for Sweden, "were actuated rather by fear than by lust of conquest or passion of faith. They wanted peace and they fought for thirty years to be sure of it. They did not learn then, and have not since, that war breeds only war."

Wolf, John B., **Louis XIV** (New York: Norton, 1968. $12.50; paperback, $3.95). It is not always possible to love him, but respect him we must: Louis XIV, king of France, the greatest of Great Powers in seventeenth-century Europe, in her age of indisputable political and cultural ascendancy. Wolf's biography of the Sun-King treats its subject on the grand scale he requires. His Louis XIV is a man who set the world spinning around him to protect the unity and power of France. He knew, says Wolf, that only a vastly strengthened monarchy could save France from the fate that had overtaken Germany, and very nearly overtook France herself during the civil wars of 1648–53. He sought virtual deification not because he was a megalomaniac but for the same reasons that "secular societies of the nineteenth and twentieth centuries have deified the state." On the whole, he was a good king, who worked hard and well, loved France, and preserved her from the machinations of squabbling aristocrats. Even those who do not share Wolf's conclusions may still agree that he has written the best biography of Louis XIV available in English.

chapter six | # The Americas

Nothing quite compares to the richness and also the rawness of life in the American hemisphere. Europe is European, Africa and Asia are almost wholly African and Asian, despite powerful recent influences from Western civilization. In the Americas, history happened differently.

If there is such a thing as "American" culture, it is a hybrid growth blending three major strains in various proportions in various parts of the hemisphere: European (British, French, Spanish, Portuguese, Dutch, German, Italian, Irish—and a little of everything else); Amerindian (in 1492 at all stages of cultural development from nomadic to urban); and African (from many parts of black Africa). At first the Amerindian population was alone. Europeans and Africans poured in during the sixteenth and seventeenth centuries until they outnumbered the Amerindians. The native stock dwindled and then recovered, but the white and black men continued to come. The races intermarried, interbred, and interacted. The American hemisphere has produced what José Vasconcelos of Mexico calls the *raza cósmica:* the cosmic race. Taking the hemisphere as a whole, it is clear that neither white man nor black man nor red man has "triumphed."

The cultures of the Americas are uneasy amalgams of all three.

American civilization is also raw. The red man was robbed of much of his traditional way of life by invading whites. He can never be the same again. The European was de-Europeanized by the unsettling experience of land rushes, gold rushes, Indian wars, waves of fresh immigration, and the struggles for independence. He is the perennial frontiersman. The African was torn from his land and resettled as the human property of European masters. Despite occasional great economic success, as in the United States, all Americans are in some sense uprooted people, in search of a meaningful past and a true identity.

The history of the Americas divides automatically into three periods—pre-Columbian, colonial, and republican. In Latin America these periods bear a startling resemblance to the ancient-medieval-modern sequence of European history. The Amerindian high cultures of Mexico and Peru compare favorably with those of Egypt and Mesopotamia. Colonial Latin America developed a feudal system not unlike that of the Middle Ages in Europe. Only since independence have a strong middle class and a modern commercial-industrial economy emerged in the major Latin countries. North America, meanwhile, took a different path. Most of its white colonists were small farmers or merchants, Amerindian influence was proportionately weaker, and after a modest start economic development proceeded much more rapidly. English-speaking America and Latin America have had many parallel experiences, but today (as always) they are two different worlds.

Our strategy in this chapter has been to review books only in pre-Columbian, Latin American, and Canadian history. Since students are adequately exposed to United States history in other courses, the U.S. field is one responsibility that the world history course can dodge. But students and teachers of world history should not totally ignore it. The U.S. experience can be tied into

many discussions of the main trends of hemispheric and world history. For an excellent bibliographical guide to the history of
● the United States, see John E. Wiltz, **Books in American History** (Bloomington, Ind.: Indiana U. P., 1964. Paperback, $1.95). It was written for high school students, teachers, and librarians, but anyone can use it as a general introduction to the best scholarly and popular literature in the field. Wiltz reviews more than four hundred titles.

Arcienegas, Germán, **Latin America:** *A Cultural History* (New York: Knopf, 1967. $7.00). A Colombian scholar who has held visiting professorships at several North American universities, Germán Arcienegas knows and loves the culture of Latin America with an almost overwhelming intimacy. His style is warm, affectionate, impressionistic. He reveals the fascinating (but confusing) variety of Latin American culture—its Indian, Negro, Iberian, French, and other racial ingredients, the separate paths of its many national histories in modern times, and the ceaseless interaction of land, trade, politics, religion, and thought. The pre-Columbian and colonial eras receive generous attention. Also striking is the Introduction, which offers a comparative overview of "the four Americas": Canada, the United States, Hispanic America, and Brazil.

Burns, E. Bradford, **A History of Brazil** (New York: Columbia, 1970. $12.50). Several good outlines of Brazilian history from colonization to the present day are now available. This one, by the young U.C.L.A. Latin Americanist E. Bradford Burns, is the most "textbookish," but it should meet the needs of anyone looking for a balanced survey of the whole sweep of Brazilian history. There are seven chapters: three on the colonial age and the achievement of independence, two on the period from 1850 to 1922, and two on modern Brazil. Burns's approach is marked by polite enthusiasm and a generally unsurprising liberal-reformist bias. For the social and economic history of Brazil, the book to read is Rollie E. Poppino, **Brazil:** *The Land and People* (New York: Oxford, 1968. $8.50; paperback, $2.95).

•   Bushnell, G. H. S., **The First Americans:** *The Pre-Columbian Civilizations* (New York: McGraw, 1968. $5.50; paperback, $2.95). *The First Americans* provides a quick tour of the cultures of pre-Columbian America, with emphasis on the most advanced societies of Mexico, Central America, and Peru. Bushnell reports the latest archeological findings, including the new chronology of pre-Columbian history disclosed by radiocarbon dating. It now appears that *Homo sapiens* did not arrive on the American hemisphere until the tenth millennium B.C. The first evidences of agriculture are contemporary with those in Europe; the earliest civilizations arose during the first millennium B.C. Although Bushnell's text is briskly authoritative, it is too brief, a fault redeemed in part by the 139 illustrations. Many of these are in glorious color.

      Freyre, Gilberto, **The Masters and the Slaves:** *A Study in the Development of Brazilian Civilization* [1933] (2nd ed., abridged; New York: Knopf, 1964. $12.50; paperback, $2.95). Gilberto Freyre, as Thomas E. Skidmore writes in *The American Historical Review,* "is the most influential living interpreter of Brazil's past. Although sharply criticized in his own country by the younger generation, his vision of a multiracial patriarchal society remains the point of departure for those seeking to understand Portuguese America." *The Masters and the Slaves* is actually the first in a series of three volumes devoted to Brazilian social history (or historical sociology) from the settlements of the sixteenth century to the outbreak of the first World War. The sequels, **The Mansions and the Shanties** [1936] and **Order and Progress** [1959] (New York: Knopf, 1963–70. $12.50 each), discuss the modernization of Brazil in the nineteenth and early twentieth centuries.

In this first volume, Freyre paints a brilliantly colored portrait of colonial society. In some ways reminiscent of the American Old South, it was a society of planters and slaves, a quasi-feudal system marked by close family ties, racial tolerance, and widespread interbreeding. Many younger scholars would disagree, but Freyre urges that Brazil from the first was a relatively color-blind society.

Gibson, Charles, **Spain in America** (New York: Harper, 1966. $7.95; Torchbooks paperback, $1.95). A volume in *The New American Nation* series, Gibson's *Spain in America* performs the almost impossible feat of compressing colonial Hispanic-American history into a book of not much more than 200 pages. Moreover, it is a very good book. The eight chapters discuss the exploration and conquest of the New World, the "encomienda" system of tributary labor, church and government, Indian relations, and imperial politics. Gibson does not subscribe to the "black legend" that Spanish rule was fiendishly inhuman, but he points out that dictatorship in modern Latin America had its roots in colonial life and institutions. "The Spanish imperial government may be understood as a repressive force or cover, under which the components of dictatorship accumulated." Every plantation owner ruling over his Indian serfs was a dictator in miniature; nothing in the colonial experience prepared the elites or the masses for popular democracy. See also J. H. Parry's **The Spanish Seaborne Empire** (New York: Knopf, 1966. $7.95), an excellent survey that stresses colonial Spanish America's maritime history; and C. H. Haring, **The Spanish Empire in America** (New York: Oxford U. P., 1947. Harbinger paperback, $3.25).

Herring, Hubert, **A History of Latin America from the Beginnings to the Present** [1955] (3rd ed., New York: Knopf, 1968. $10.95). Since its first appearance in 1955, Herring's college textbook of Latin American history has become the leader in a crowded field, much respected for its painstaking thoroughness, clarity, and accuracy. The latest edition runs to more than a thousand pages. The numerous maps by Theodore R. Miller are superb. Herring divides his subject into eleven large sections, the first three on the colonial period, the rest devoted to a country-by-country survey of modern history with especially full treatment of Mexico, Brazil, and Argentina. Other good one-volume histories are available, by J. Fred Rippy, Donald M. Dozer, and E. Bradford Burns.

Humphreys, R. A., and John Lynch, eds., **The Origins of the Latin American Revolutions, 1808–1826** (New York: Knopf, 1965. $4.50; paperback, $2.95). The political liberation of Latin America from Iberian rule began not with shots "heard round the world" but with the exploits of Napoleon Bonaparte, who occupied Spain and Portugal in 1807–08. The Portuguese king fled to Brazil, the Spanish king abdicated, and revolution in the Spanish-American colonies at first took the form of resistance to the authority of Napoleon and the puppet-king of French-occupied Spain, the Emperor's brother Joseph. In time the smoldering hostility of American-born settlers toward the *peninsulares* (Iberian-born), who held most of the highest offices in colonial administration, precipitated a final break with the home countries, but the revolutions of 1808–26 differed in many ways from the American Revolution and from each other. Humphreys and Lynch have given us in this attractive volume a selection of short essays, chiefly by modern scholars, on the causes of the revolutions. The authors canvass the role of the Enlightenment, the Jesuits, foreign powers, imperial administration, economic interests, resentment against the *peninsulares,* and nationalism. A separate section contains essays on the Brazilian experience, where independence came peacefully.

McNaught, Kenneth, **The History of Canada** (New York: Praeger, 1970. $9.00; Penguin paperback, $1.95). The world's third largest country in area, with a population of twenty million people and a more or less American standard of living, Canada has lived such a quiet and respectable life that world historians often ignore it. In all fairness, any historian has a job on his hands making Canadian history either exciting or exotic to the non-Canadian reader. McNaught does as well as anyone. His maps are good, and he addresses himself perceptively to the age-old problem of Canada's search for national integration and identity. In a concluding chapter, he speculates that the Canadian experiment "has roots that now are probably deep enough to sustain a tolerant federalism against the storms of the future." See also J. Bartlet Brebner's longer but somewhat less imaginative **Canada:** *A Modern History* [1960] (rev. ed., Ann Arbor, Mich.: U. of Michigan Press, 1970. $10.00) and Mason Wade, **The French Canadians, 1760–1967** [1955] (2 vols., rev. ed.; New York: St. Martin's, 1968. $25.00 the set).

Masur, Gerhard, **Simon Bolivar** [1948] (rev. ed., Albuquerque: U. of New Mexico Press, 1969. $15.00). "One of the outstanding figures of the nineteenth century and one of the great personalities of all time," Simón Bolívar is the man most revered by Latin Americans today, a folk-hero more beloved than George Washington by North Americans, a romantic and paradoxical figure whose military triumphs over Spanish armies ensured the liberation of most of South America, a lover of freedom who ruled his people after independence with an iron hand, believing them unready for true democracy. Gerhard Masur views Bolívar with loving enthusiasm in this comprehensive biography. Only in blindness to the need for basic socioeconomic change, a blindness shared by almost everyone else in the early nineteenth century in Latin America, did Bolívar fall seriously short. In all other ways, Masur finds him worthy of the hero-worship he has long received.

Morison, Samuel Eliot, **Christopher Columbus, Mariner** (Boston: Little, 1955. $5.95; Mentor paperback, $0.60). A

Harvard historian with a special interest in naval and maritime history, Morison is also a sailor in his own right. This book is the happy result of his decision to write a life of Columbus only after he himself had sailed the routes of Columbus's voyages to the New World in ships comparable to the great Genoese mariner's. This he did, during the Harvard Columbus Expeditions of 1939 and 1940, learning much that armchair biographers inevitably miss. In 1942 he brought out a two-volume scholarly biography of Columbus, entitled **Admiral of the Ocean Sea,** and a one-volume abridgement with the same title (Boston: Little, 1942. $15.00), which won the Pulitzer Prize for Biography. *Christopher Columbus, Mariner* is a severely shortened and rewritten version of the longer works.

The purpose of all of them is summed up in the preface to the first: "Although I have not neglected the problems connected with the nationality, birth, early life and objectives of Columbus, the emphasis in this book is on what he did, where he went, and what sort of seaman he was." Morison hails his hero as "the greatest navigator of his age," "a failure as a colonial administrator," but the man who did "more to direct the course of history than any individual since Augustus Caesar."

Parry, J. H., and P. M. Sherlock, **A Short History of the West Indies** [1956] (3rd ed., New York: St. Martin's, 1971. $12.00; paperback, $5.95). Few parts of the world are as poor in historical tradition, cultural identity, and sense of common cause as the islands of the Caribbean Sea. The unwarlike aboriginal inhabitants proved unable to withstand the European invasions and became nearly extinct within a century. Their place was taken by transplanted Europeans and Africans, but the islands were too small, too dependent on European markets, too much under the heel of rival Western great powers, and too isolated from one another to develop until quite recently the independent spirit that arose throughout the rest of the Americas in the eighteenth and early nineteenth centuries. "West Indian history," write Parry and Sherlock, "appears disjointed and unreal to West Indians today. It is a story told from someone else's point of view."

But the authors have made the best of an admittedly difficult business in this well constructed history of Cuba, Jamaica, Hispaniola (now the Dominican Republic and Haiti), Puerto Rico, and the smaller Caribbean islands. The centuries of colonial rule are emphasized, with somewhat more attention to the British West Indies than to the Spanish and French.

Peterson, Frederick A., **Ancient Mexico:** *An Introduction to the Pre-Hispanic Cultures* (New York: Putnam, 1959. Capricorn paperback, $3.25). Many North Americans and Europeans equate ancient Mexico with the empire of the Aztecs, which is roughly the same thing as reducing ancient history to the history of the Roman empire after Constantine. There were many civilized peoples in ancient Mexico, both before and during the Aztec era. Over 5,000 sites have been worked by archeologists. The "classic period," as defined by Frederick A. Peterson, lasted from approximately 150 B.C. to 900 A.D. and included the urbanized societies of the Olmecs, Maya, Totonacs, and Zapotecs. Teotihuacán, near Mexico City, was also built during this period. A "post-classical" period followed, marked by the somewhat inferior achievements of the Toltecs, Mixtecs, and—at the very end—Aztecs. Peterson adopts a topical approach that gives him many opportunities to study these peoples comparatively. "America," he insists, "was easily on a par with Europe. Several million Indians were killed to prove that Europeans were more civilized."

●   Prescott, W. H., **The Conquest of Mexico and the Conquest of Peru** [1843–47] (New York: Modern Library. $4.95; abridged ed., Washington Square paperback, $1.45). William Hickling Prescott (1796–1859) was America's first great world historian, a prose artist with a mastery of the romantic style of narrative history that few of his countrymen have ever equaled. These histories of the conquest of Mexico by Cortez and of Peru by Pizarro are classics that still compel respect.

Sauer, Carl Ortwin, **The Early Spanish Main** (Berkeley: U. of California Press, 1966. $9.50; paperback, $2.45). Spain's first American empire was not the Mexico of Cortez or the Peru of Pizarro but the West Indies of Christopher Columbus. In this book, a specialist in historical geography gives us a learned and moving account of how this empire was won, and for all practical purposes lost, with the virtual destruction of the whole native population. "By 1519," Sauer writes, "the Spanish main was a sorry shell." The villain of at least the first act of this tragedy, he contends, was Columbus himself, a helpless victim of gold fever. "The course of Spanish empire was first turned to its fateful search for gold by the *idée fixe* that dominated Columbus."

Scobie, James R., **Argentina:** *A City and a Nation* [1964] (2nd ed., New York: Oxford U. P., 1971. $7.50; paperback, $2.50). Scobie rejects the conventional political and cultural approaches to Latin American history in favor of an economic emphasis. He reviews the history of Argentina from earliest times, in a series of topical chapters on such subjects as the growth of Buenos Aires, agriculture on the Pampas, and industrialization. There is a very extensive and useful bibliography.

● Simpson, Lesley Byrd, **Many Mexicos** [1941] (4th ed., Berkeley: U. of California Press, 1966. $10.00; paperback, $2.45). "We have too many roots, we have too many pasts. The history of Mexico is like those pre-Columbian pyramids on which new races built other pyramids, and afterward other races built still more." So says the poet Octavio Paz, adding that "Mexico has still not succeeded in combining its past into one real past." Both Indian and Spanish, divided by geography and climate into many sharply contrasting regions, Mexico is not an easy country for outsiders to know well. Simpson relates its history in brief biographical sketches and thematic essays that display wit, eloquence, and deep understanding of the Mexican past. The author is opinionated, but never dull. *Many Mexicos* deserves its many editions. For the development of the Mexican economy, another valuable book is Charles C. Cumberland, **Mexico:** *The Struggle for Modernity* (New York: Oxford U.P., 1968. $8.50; paperback, $2.95).

Thompson, J. Eric S., **The Rise and Fall of Maya Civilization** [1954] (2nd ed., Norman, Okla.: U. of Oklahoma Press, 1966. $5.95). A leading specialist in Maya archeology, Eric Thompson opens his book with a vivid account of his first visit some forty years ago to Tikal, in Guatemala, the largest of the Maya ruins, and the most beautiful memorial to ancient Indian civilization in the hemisphere. Surrounded by almost impenetrable jungle, Tikal reminds us that the Maya are the only people known to world history whose civilization "developed and reached maturity in thickly forested tropics." After three chapters on the geography, anthropology, and history of Maya civilization, Thompson examines its intellectual and artistic achievement, its ways of life, religion, and place in history. Unlike the other Amerindian peoples, the Maya developed an elaborate system of writing, comparable to Egyptian hieroglyphics. Although most of the "glyphs" or characters are undecipherable, scholars can read a few, and they also have at their disposal several works from the sixteenth to eighteenth centuries by natives who wrote in Mayan, using the Western alphabet. But the "classic" period of Maya history dates back to the years 200–925 A.D. The culture encountered by the Spaniards was in a "decadent" phase; Maya civilization had already "fallen." *The Rise and Fall of Maya Civilization* is both a work of impeccable scholarship and a popularization better written than the books of most popularizers.

Womack, John, Jr., **Zapata and the Mexican Revolution** (New York: Knopf, 1969. $10.00; Vintage paperback, $2.95). This no doubt deserves its reputation as one of the finest "first books" ever written in any field of history. The author is a young Harvard historian and former Rhodes Scholar who refuses to oversimplify. The hero of his book is not so much the great revolutionary himself as the country people of his home state of Morelos in south-central Mexico, the *campesinos* who had been ignored by the ruling classes throughout the nineteenth century and who tried to take matters into their own hands in the decade after 1910, with men like Emiliano Zapata as their freely chosen leaders. The rural reforms instituted by Mexican governments after the fall of Díaz owed much to their militance; and yet nothing was ever really settled, and many of the hopes of the *campesinos* went unfulfilled. Womack avoids catch-all sociological generalizations, preferring to let the complex and dramatic evidence speak—more or less!—for itself. In Womack's own words, his book is "not an analysis but a story because the truth of the revolution in Morelos is in the feeling of it."

chapter seven | Africa and Australasia

A disconcertingly large number of Americans still believe that Africa south of the Sahara has no history or civilization of her own, apart from the exploits of white invaders. For these Americans, black Africa before the European partition consisted exclusively of small tribes of naked illiterate savages eking out a meager existence in jungles and bush country, saved from timeless misery by the arrival of Western civilization.

The strong interest in African history awakened by the liberation of African peoples from European rule since the second World War has resulted in the appearance of an extensive scholarly and popular literature that exposes the absurdity of this view of the African past. Although a few native African peoples have clung to what may fairly be called a prehistoric way of life, the great majority have been undergoing more or less continuous cultural evolution along the same lines as other races for thousands of years.

Indigenous black African civilizations with town life, imperial governments, agriculture, metal-working, and most of the other indices of advanced culture, flourished in several parts of the continent during Europe's Middle Ages. Progress was especially rapid between about 1000 and 1500 A.D. For various reasons (including the debilitating effects of the Atlantic slave trade) Africa has developed more slowly than Europe in recent centuries, but throughout most of the Christian era the black populations of Africa and the white populations of northern Europe were advancing at much the same rate and in much the same directions.

In this chapter we shall review books in sub-Saharan African history from antiquity to 1945. At the end of the chapter we list a few books on the history of Australasia (Australia, New Zealand, and the islands of the southwestern Pacific). Australasia, too, had indigenous populations when the white man arrived, but their numbers were significantly smaller, their cultures were less highly developed, and little is known of their premodern history. Australasian history remains primarily a chronicle of European colonization.

• Bovill, E. W., **The Golden Trade of the Moors** [1958] (2nd ed., New York: Oxford U. P., 1968. $10.25; Galaxy paperback, $2.25). This is a revised and expanded version of Bovill's earlier book, *Caravans of the Old Sahara* [1933], written to show "how the trans-Saharan trade routes had woven ties of blood and culture between the peoples north and south of the desert." The new book differs chiefly in the relatively larger attention given to the impact of trans-Saharan trade and politics on the peoples of North Africa. But in both versions "the land to which every thread in my story leads" is the Sudan—not the present-day Sudanese republic, which occupies only the extreme eastern part of the Sudan, but a great historic region of black Africa that extends south of the Sahara from the Atlantic Ocean to the Nile basin and includes the territory of the now independent states of Mauritania, Mali, Upper Volta, Niger, and Chad.

The author describes in colorful detail the rise and fall of the medieval Sudanese empires of Ghana, Mali, and Songhai, the Moroccan empire of the Almoravid Berbers, and the trade in Sudanese gold that helped to make such states possible. The trans-Saharan caravan routes continued to flourish well into the nineteenth century, when they were finally replaced by rail transport and oceanic trade with the European colonial powers.

Crowder, Michael, **West Africa under Colonial Rule** (Evanston, Ill.: Northwestern U. P., 1968. $10.00) Several years ago when Michael Crowder lectured on West African colonialism to officers of the Royal Sierra Leone Military Force, "the one British officer present . . . stood stiffly at attention during question-time and demanded that I withdraw what he considered my anti-British remarks; by contrast, the African officers for the most part considered my criticisms of colonial rule very tame." Whether fierce or tame, Crowder's book lends support to the argument of many present-day Africans that the political seizure of their continent by European powers in the late nineteenth century did little for Africa that Africans were not quite capable of doing for themselves. In the French and British colonies of West Africa, to which this study is limited, Crowder contends that modernization would have occurred without foreign rule; in some respects, modernization was powerfully impeded by the policies of the occupying powers. *West Africa under Colonial Rule* includes a detailed history of the European annexations and a careful analysis of colonial administration in theory and practice, the colonial economy, and social change during the colonial period. Four concluding chapters study the beginnings of African nationalist politics to 1945.

• Davidson, Basil, **Africa in History:** *Themes and Outlines* (New York: Macmillan, 1969. $6.95; Collier paperback, $2.95). Journalist, traveler, novelist, and popularizer of African studies, Basil Davidson has done more than any other living writer to introduce African history to the general reading public.

Although he is not a scholar by profession, his scholarship is better than that of many academicians; and his literary powers are exceptional. He is also a prominent representative of the movement in African studies that seeks to dispel the popular image of black Africans as peoples without a history of their own, as passive beneficiaries of the "higher" cultures of Egypt, Asia, and Europe.

Africa in History sweeps from the Stone Age to the present in just over 300 pages. Its pro-African bias is obvious, but never fanatical. The author traces generally steady upward development for most of the indigenous population of the continent to the African "Middle Ages" in the fifteenth and sixteenth centuries, followed by debilitating contact with movements in the outside world, and then rebirth in the second half of the twentieth century. At a somewhat more leisurely pace, much of the same ground is covered in Davidson's **A History of West Africa to the Nineteenth Century,** with F. K. Buah (Garden City, N.Y.: Doubleday, 1966. Anchor paperback, $1.95); and **A History of East and Central Africa, to the Late Nineteenth Century,** with J. E. F. Mhina (Garden City, N.Y.: Doubleday, 1969. Anchor paperback, $2.50).

Davidson, Basil, **The African Genius:** *An Introduction to African Cultural and Social History* (Boston: Little, 1969. $7.95; paperback, $2.75). "This book," writes Basil Davidson, "is about a new synthesis of cultural patterns and values that has lately begun to emerge from the labour of many workers in several disciplines, and notably in social anthropology." In place of orthodox chronological history, Davidson sums up recent research on the "social charters" and "structures of belief" of traditional black African culture. He also studies the "mechanisms of change" that have modified and in some ways overwhelmed African culture during the past thousand years.

Today, Davidson writes, Africa needs to be "modernized," but even more she needs new structures of social life and belief that are "nourished by the vigour and resilience of native genius, by all the inheritance of self-respect and innovating confidence that has carried these peoples through past centuries of change and cultural expansion." *The African Genius,* as another African specialist, Roland Oliver, comments, is "the most serious and best integrated of all [Davidson's] books." No one interested in Africa can fail to learn from it.

•   Davidson, Basil, **Black Mother:** *The Years of the African Slave Trade* (Boston: Little, 1961. $8.50; as **The African Slave Trade:** *Pre-Colonial History, 1450–1850,* paperback, $2.45). Davidson's purpose in this book is to explain the nature of Afro-European relations in the four centuries before the European partition of the continent, with special attention to the slave trade. Some fifty million blacks were sold into slavery during this period, although many of these unfortunates never reached their destinations alive. Davidson shows that for the most part this was a peaceful trade between Western slavers and the chiefs of native African coastal states, who moved quickly to seal off the interior of the continent and prevent any European encroachment on their sources of supply. But he argues that the trade did Africa almost irreparable harm, by bolstering the rule of the most reactionary feudal elements in native African society, and by bringing stagnation and even decay to the African economy. It was a moral, social, political, and economic disaster from which the continent is only beginning to recover in our time. For a more detailed and popularized treatment of the slave trade, see Daniel P. Mannix and Malcolm Cowley, **Black Cargoes:** *A History of the Atlantic Slave Trade, 1518–1865* (New York: Viking, 1962. $6.50; Compass paperback, $1.85).

•   Davidson, Basil, **The Lost Cities of Africa** [1959] (rev. ed., Boston: Little, 1970. $8.50; paperback, $2.45). The European explorers of Africa in the nineteenth century had little respect for the "savages" they met there, but Africa was, after all, a vast unexplored continent and no one could be quite sure what lost civilizations or fabulous ruins waited to be found in its hinterlands. The romantic imagination was stirred especially by the discovery in 1869 in southern Rhodesia of Great Zimbabwe, a ruined stone city with walls thirty feet high. In *The Lost Cities of Africa,* Basil Davidson attempts to reconstruct the history of Great Zimbabwe and the Bantu culture that flourished in southeastern Africa as early as the sixth century A.D. He also investigates several other indigenous sub-Saharan cultures that became urbanized without European aid. Among his "lost cities" are Meroë, part of the ancient Kushite kingdom founded by Egyptian colonists in the Sudan; Timbuktu, a great market town and center of Islamic learning in the Mali and Songhai empires of western Africa; and such merchant cities of the southeastern coast as Kilwa and Mombasa. In effect, this is a general survey of the history of sub-Saharan Africa.

July, Robert W., **A History of the African People** (New York: Scribner, 1970. $15.00; paperback, $5.95). This handsomely illustrated textbook of sub-Saharan African history presents a clearly organized and well written account of the African people themselves, with minimal attention to the European influence. Part One, "Ancient Africa," traces the development of black Africa to the close of the eighteenth century. Part Two, "Modern Africa," follows it into the post-independence era.

Moorehead, Alan, **The White Nile** (New York: Harper, 1961. $6.95; deluxe ed., $15.00). Here is the Africa of modern Western legend and romance. Moorehead does not miss a single chance: his pages are thickly populated with sadistic black chieftains, groaning slaves, brilliant (but eccentric) white explorers, crafty Arab merchants, howling dervishes, cowardly Egyptians, and steel-nerved British generals. Speke reaches the source of the Nile, Stanley finds Livingstone, Kitchener avenges Gordon. In this popular history of the European exploration and seizure of the White Nile, from the Burton-Speke expedition of 1856 to the British reconquest of the Sudan in 1898, Alan Moorehead is clearly guilty of sensationalism, but it is all very readable stuff, based on the voluminous writings of the explorers themselves. Their point of view, rather than the African, usually prevails.

● See also Moorehead's **The Blue Nile** (New York: Harper, 1962. $15.00; Dell paperback. $0.60).

Oliver, Roland, and John D. Fage, **A Short History of Africa** [1962] (3rd ed., Baltimore: Penguin, 1970. Paperback, $1.45). Although the first edition of this book appeared little more than ten years ago, it is already regarded as a "classic" in the field, one of the first attempts by scholars to survey the history of the whole continent from earliest times. The level of interpretative insight is consistently high, but the authors are sometimes defeated by the sheer variety of the African historical experience. Perhaps the greatest structural weakness of the book is its failure to focus on the African peoples themselves; disproportionate attention is given to external influences. But Oliver and Fage are not sneering Eurocentrists of the old school. After the sixteenth century, they point out, Africa fell behind Europe in various respects, but "it was in large measure the progress already made by the Africans in earlier centuries that enabled them to resist the modern age for so long."

Robinson, Ronald, and John Gallagher, with Alice Denny, **Africa and the Victorians:** *The Climax of Imperialism in the Dark Continent* (New York: St. Martin's, 1961. Anchor paperback, $4.50). Most explanations of European (and especially British) imperialism in Africa in the nineteenth century stress the arrogance of nineteenth-century European culture, the zeal of missionaries and explorers, the greed of business interests, and the thirst of the public for imperial glory in an otherwise peaceful era. Robinson and Gallagher maintain that none of these things explains the commitment of European armed might to the partition of Africa. By the time the partition actually took place, most segments of the British public had lost interest in African matters, and it is therefore to "the official mind" that scholars must look for "the main explanation of what happened." But even British officialdom was not originally bent on imperial conquest in Africa: its hand was forced, say Robinson and Gallagher, by events in Africa itself, chiefly by the challenge of militant Afrikaner nationalism in the southern part of the continent and by the threat to the Indian trade routes posed by the collapse of the Khedivial regime in Egypt in 1882. When Britain and France assumed power in Egypt, to protect the Suez Canal, they set in motion the "scramble" that led in just a few years to European seizure of the whole continent.

Grattan, C. Hartley, **The Southwest Pacific:** *A Modern History* (2 vols., Ann Arbor, Mich.: U. of Michigan, 1963. $7.50 and $10.00). The Southwest Pacific of this imposing two-volume set by C. Hartley Grattan includes a continent, thousands of islands big and small, and a generous slice of the world's largest ocean: an area averaging six thousand miles wide and long. Because of its low population density and remoteness from the centers of civilization, the Southwest Pacific is often ignored by historians, but it does have a history, some of which deserves attention in any world history course.

Grattan's first volume recounts the European reconnaissance of the area in early modern times, the establishment of Australia and New Zealand as British colonies, the beginnings of Antarctic exploration, and the complex history of the island groups of Polynesia, Melanesia, and Micronesia, visited for many years by Western seafarers and partitioned by Britain, France, Germany, and the United States in the nineteenth century. The second volume begins with the federation of the six Australian colonies into a single commonwealth in 1901 and follows its history and that of New Zealand, the islands, and Antarctic exploration to 1960. Grattan has something to say about black and brown native populations, but essentially this is "a story of how 'the West' became established in the Southwest Pacific," a story of white explorers and settlers by an American who has devoted most of his life to Pacific studies. See also Douglas Pike, **Australia:** *The Quiet Continent* [1962] (2nd ed., New York: Cambridge U. P., 1970. $12.50; paperback, $2.45).

●   Moorehead, Alan, **The Fatal Impact:** *An Account of the Invasion of the South Pacific* (New York: Harper, 1966. $6.95). Captain James Cook (1728–1779) made three historic voyages to the South Pacific, which helped to open the islands, New Zealand, and the eastern coast of Australia to white colonization. The white man brought to the South Pacific not only his culture but also ecological devastation that changed the whole face of Australasian life, both human and animal. Moorehead (Australian born himself) describes the effects of this "fatal impact," beginning with a fascinating account of Cook's voyages. He devotes most of his attention to Tahiti, Australia, and the Antarctic region. Like all his books, it makes easy reading.

chapter eight | # Modern Europe, 1789-1945

Most of the disagreement about whether an age, a country, an idea, an artifact, an institution, or a man deserves to be called "modern" would dissolve if scholars reached a working consensus on the meaning of modernity. The word itself has no substantive content. The Latin *modernus* comes from *modo,* "just now." In this literal meaning, something is modern that is happening "just now," something that belongs to "our" time. In the days of Moses, the Ten Commandments were modern. In the fourteenth century, knights in shining armor were modern. Today, one might argue that steam locomotives, dirigibles, and ice boxes are not modern.

We shall examine in this chapter books in the history of Europe from the outbreak of the French Revolution to the end of the second World War. In my view, this is the beginning of the "modern" period in European history, the period in which European civilization leaped forward to a level and kind of life wholly without precedent in world history. European civilization changed so fast that it also pulled segments of the traditional societies of Asia, Africa, and the Americas into the "modern" age. In a few instances (such as the United States, Canada, Japan) non-European countries have actually equaled or outstripped Europe in the degree of their "modernization."

But we are talking now about a "modernity" that involves much more than the accident of happening in "our" time. Just as the word "progress" has come to mean "improvement" when it originally meant only "forward motion," so the word "modern" has come to denote a particular kind of society, which arrived in western Europe a certain number of years ago, depending on one's reading of the events, and may ultimately give way to some other kind of society.

I have already, in the introduction to Chapter Five, identified what I think are the three major components of this new society: industrialization, democracy, and globalization. In other words, a modern society is one that has largely replaced human labor with machine labor, shifted the balance of power and wealth from kings and elites to the broad masses, and interacted with other societies to form an interdependent world community. Something may properly be called modern if it belongs to, and harmonizes with, this new social order. The new order is also characterized by secularism and individualism—it divorces church from state and assigns a higher priority to personal development than to the preservation of social discipline and routine. But the demand for religious and personal liberty often clashes with the needs of industrial democracy, and in a showdown between the two, liberty generally loses. Much as I would prefer to believe that secularism and individualism are indispensable ingredients of a modern social order, I am afraid that the facts of modern history do not support my wishes.

It should also go without saying that Europe did not become modern on July 14, 1789, or at any other precise point in time. No European country, for that matter, is entirely modern even today. The revolution of modernity, of global industrial democracy, still goes on, and is still far from complete. The industrial thrust of the revolution began in late eighteenth-century England; the democratic thrust began in late eighteenth-century France; and globalization began near the close of the nineteenth century when the Western impact on Russia, Asia, and Africa resulted in the rapid decline and fall of their traditional social orders. But every country retains powerful elements of its traditional life. The machine has not yet completely abolished physical toil. Old and new "power elites" hinder the advance of democracy. Globalization is frustrated by the persistence of provincial loyalties. Modernity is an expensive and sometimes lethal luxury. At the same time, the headlong pace of change since 1789 makes one doubt that anything, except a thermonuclear holocaust or the exhaustion of nature herself, can halt its progress.

● Ashton, T. S., **The Industrial Revolution:** *1760–1830* (New York: Oxford U. P., 1948. Paperback, $1.25). You may quarrel about whether it was an "industrial" revolution, or a "revolution" at all, whether the conventional dates of 1760–1830 really apply, and whether it was the first such revolution, or one of a series in world history, but the fact remains that something happened in the economic history of Great Britain between the middle of the eighteenth and the middle of the nineteenth centuries that turned the world upside down. This brief book by an economic historian explains how and why such a revolution took place. Among the causative forces were the progress of agriculture, an accumulation of capital ripe for investment, a rising labor supply, the presence in eighteenth-century society of energetic entrepreneurs free to try their luck, and a mental climate that encouraged technological innovation. On the whole, Ashton thinks, the Industrial Revolution immediately benefited rich and poor alike. The standard of living went up, and a population already soaring before the revolution began was adequately fed, while next door the people of industrially undeveloped Ireland starved or fled abroad.

Barzun, Jacques, **Classic, Romantic and Modern** [1943] (rev. ed., Boston: Little, 1961. $5.95; Anchor paperback, $1.45). Originally entitled *Romanticism and the Modern Ego,* this little book sums up Barzun's thoughts about the place of romanticism in modern cultural history. Barzun sees romanticism as a liberating, popular, and creative force in early nineteenth-century life. The French Revolution and Napoleon, along with the savage self-criticism of the Enlightenment by its own philosophers, had swept away the classical culture of aristocratic Europe. The romantics sought "to create a new world on the ruins of the old . . . in the knowledge that man is both creative and limited, a doer and a sufferer, infinite in spirit and finite in action." Barzun is also the author of **Darwin, Marx, Wagner:** *Critique of a Heritage* [1941] (2nd ed., Garden City, N.Y.: Doubleday, 1958. Anchor paperback, $1.95), which attacks all three men as subverters of romanticism, who sought to replace its liberal ideals with a soulless animal determinism.

Baumer, Franklin L., **Religion and the Rise of Scepticism** (New York: Harcourt, 1960. Harbinger paperback, $2.45). From the perspective of intellectual history, the hallmark of "modernity" is the abandonment of religious faith by most of the thinking people in our society, a desertion much more obvious in the European context than in the American. Belief has been replaced by a corrosive scepticism that not only denies the old creeds but attacks the possibility of faith itself. The rise and hardening of this "sceptical tradition" into a new orthodoxy is the subject of a deeply impressive book by the Yale intellectual historian Franklin L. Baumer. Most of it is devoted to unbelief (and the agonized search for new faith) in the nineteenth and twentieth centuries, but Baumer also delves into the origins of scepticism in the thought of the Renaissance, the Scientific Revolution, and the Enlightenment. Voltaire and Hume, Comte and Mill, Nietzsche and Freud are all here, together with scores of other modern minds, including such relatively smaller fry as Aldous Huxley,

C. E. M. Joad, and Arthur Koestler, whose books have much to tell us about the spiritual temper of our time.

Berlin, Sir Isaiah, **Karl Marx:** *His Life and Environment* [1939] (3rd ed., New York: Oxford, 1963. Galaxy paperback, $1.95). Even those who find Marxism repellent can hardly deny that it has been one of the two or three most influential social philosophies of the last hundred years. Berlin's short biography of Marx is crisp, authoritative, and brilliantly written. He puts his deep knowledge of political theory to good use in analyzing the sources of Marx's world-view and in explaining what Marx himself taught. A lively history of both Marxist and non-Marxist socialism is Edmund Wilson's **To the Finland Station** [1940] (rev. ed., New York: Farrar, 1972. $15.00; Anchor paperback, $2.95).

Brinton, Crane, **The Anatomy of Revolution** [1938] (New York: Random. Vintage paperback, $1.95). Brinton supplies in this popular book a comparative study of one type of modern political revolution, the revolution that promises liberation from tyranny in the name of freedom and equality. His four examples of democratic revolutions are the English of the 1640's and 1650's, the American of the 1770's and 1780's, the French of the 1780's and 1790's, and the Russian of 1917–24. "When all necessary concessions are made to those who insist that events in history are unique, it remains true that the four revolutions we have studied do display some striking uniformities."

•   Bullock, Alan, **Hitler:** *A Study in Tyranny* [1953] (rev. ed., New York: Harper, 1964. $10.00; Torchbooks paperback, $4.75; abridged ed., Perennial paperback, $1.50). Adolf Hitler may have been the worst man who ever lived. But one does not earn such a distinction easily, and understanding the man who earned it is a formidable task. The best political biography of Hitler is Alan Bullock's. Because of the central position of Hitler in the history of the National Socialist party and, after

1933, of National Socialist Germany, this book doubles as a history of the Third Reich. Bullock does not sell Hitler short. By at least 1938 "he exercised arbitrary rule over Germany to a degree rarely, if ever, equalled in a modern industrialized State." At the same time, he won an empire comparable to Napoleon's. Only in a country as strong as Germany could Hitler have gone so far, but he alone "provided the indispensable leadership, the flair for grasping opportunities, the boldness in using them. . . . It took the combined efforts of the three most powerful nations in the world to break his hold on Europe." This is not the last word on Hitler, or the Third Reich, but Bullock has done his job with thoroughness, accuracy, and perception. Further light is shed in David Schoenbaum, **Hitler's Social Revolution:** *Class and Status in Nazi Germany, 1933–1939* (Garden City, N.Y.: Doubleday, 1966. Anchor paperback, $1.95), and Richard Grunberger, **The Twelve-Year Reich:** *A Social History of Nazi Germany* (New York: Holt, 1971. $10.00; Ballantine paperback, $1.95). Of less value is William L. Shirer's best-seller, **The Rise and Fall of the Third Reich** (New York: Simon, 1960. $12.50; Crest paperback, $1.95).

• Collier, Richard, **Duce!** *A Biography of Benito Mussolini* (New York: Viking, 1971. $12.50; Popular Library paperback, $1.25). Insecure, bumptious, and vacillating, Mussolini bobbed to the top of Italian politics through a mixture of shrewd opportunism and acting ability. He then led his country into a disastrous alliance with Nazi Germany that ruined him and very nearly ruined Italy. Like most biographies of Mussolini, *Duce!* is more a work of journalism than of history. It is flashy, entertaining, and extensively researched. Collier and his many assistants reportedly traveled 200,000 miles to gather their materials, and interviewed hundreds of people who lived through the Fascist epoch. The Mussolini who comes to view in their work was a far cry from the Great Man he impersonated.

Deutscher, Isaac, **Stalin:** *A Political Biography* [1948] (2nd ed., New York: Oxford, 1967. $13.50; Galaxy paperback, $3.95). No one is ever likely to succeed in making a glamorous or romantic figure of Joseph V. Stalin. The late Isaac Deutscher was not about to try. A former Communist, born in Poland, Deutscher was one of the wisest students of Soviet history in the Western world, but he admired Leon Trotsky too profoundly to be able to treat Stalin with anything like warmth. The secret of Stalin's astonishing rise to power in Soviet Russia, Deutscher contends, was his mastery of the details of party management. "Like none of his colleagues, he was immersed in the party's daily drudgery and in all its kitchen cabals." Once installed in power, he guided the Soviet nation through its second Bolshevik revolution, the forced industrialization and collectivization of the post-1929 era. Later, he led Russia to victory in World War Two over the legions of international fascism. But throughout, he remained a mediocre man, of limited intelligence, without ideas of his own, a party hack armed with total power, who never swerved from using it, heedless of the costs. Despite its strongly anti-Stalin bias, this remains an important study of the dictator's rise to power. Deutscher has also written a three-volume biography of his hero Trotsky; see especially the first volume, **The Prophet Armed:** *Trotsky, 1879–1921* (New York: Oxford, 1954. $10.95; Vintage paperback, $2.45).

Eyck, Erich, **Bismarck and the German Empire** [1941–44] (abridged ed., New York: Macmillan, 1950. Norton paperback, $1.95). A political refugee from the Third Reich, Erich Eyck sought in his studies of Bismarck some of the nineteenth-century sources for the weakness of German liberalism. Admitting that the results of Bismarck's actions were "more far-reaching than those of any other statesman of his time," Eyck nevertheless saw Bismarck as the agent of a disastrous transformation "of the spirit and mentality of the German people." The ruthless methods he employed to unify and rule Germany left the German people ill prepared to govern themselves or behave responsibly in the world community after his departure from public life. "Under Bismarck's leadership the German nation had become united, strong, and powerful. But the sense of freedom and individual independence, of justice and humanity, had been lamentably weakened by the politics of power and of material interest and by the personal régime which the Iron Chancellor had imposed upon his countrymen."

Falls, Cyril, **The Great War:** *1914–1918* (New York: Putnam, 1959. Capricorn paperback, $3.25). Cyril Falls fought in the first World War, on the British side, and spent most of the rest of his life studying its history. He wrote this book not only to provide an accurate account of what happened but also to "show what the war had meant to my generation . . . to commemorate the spirit in which these men served and fought."

For all the killing and suffering caused by the war, it was not in Falls's judgment a cynical affair. The soldiers of every army fought bravely, patriotically, with purity of motive and little cruelty. Nor can he accept the familiar postwar "myth" that "the military art stood still." On the contrary, "most of the belligerents . . . threw up leaders notable for skill and character" and numerous technical innovations made a difference in the fighting. This anti-debunking approach is bound to irritate some of his readers, but one thing is certain. *The Great War* is great military history. It covers all the fronts, on the land, in the sea, and in the air, and it is beautifully written. Also, do not miss Barbara Tuchman's

● Pulitzer prizewinner, **The Guns of August** (New York: Macmillan, 1962. $8.95; Dell paperback, $1.25), an absorbing account of the decisive opening weeks of war in 1914.

Greene, John C., **The Death of Adam:** *Evolution and Its Impact on Western Thought* (Ames, Iowa: Iowa State U. P., 1959. Paperback, $2.95). This is a careful study of the origins of evolutionary thought in the history of science from the late seventeenth century to the middle of the nineteenth. Although Charles Darwin deserves credit for the theory of evolution by natural selection, Greene shows that he could not have developed it without the earlier speculation and research of men such as Robert Hooke, the comte de Buffon, James Hutton, Charles Lyell, Jean de Lamarck—and his own grandfather Erasmus Darwin. See also Loren C. Eiseley, **Darwin's Century:** *Evolution and the Men Who Discovered It* (Garden City, N.Y.: Doubleday, 1958. Anchor paperback, $2.50), and Gertrude Himmelfarb, **Darwin and the Darwinian Revolution** (Garden City, N.Y.: Doubleday, 1959. Norton paperback, $2.95).

Harcave, Sidney, **Years of the Golden Cockerel:** *The Last Romanov Tsars, 1814–1917* (New York: Macmillan, 1968. $12.50). Harcave borrows his title from Pushkin's fable about a ruthless tsar whose kingdom is guarded by the magic of a golden cockerel. In the end, the bird pecks his ungrateful master to death. Russia under the last Romanovs, Harcave suggests, was a land not unlike that of the poet's tale. Although the collapse of Romanov Russia cannot be blamed on her tsars alone, their deeds counted for something. "Their freedom was limited, and, as the years passed, it narrowed. Yet the manner in which they exercised it, their motivations, their intentions were factors in determining the fate of the dynasty and the monarchy." Regrettably for the Russia they sought to preserve, they lived too much in the shadow of the past. Despite good intentions, each of the last five tsars "led the dynasty a step closer to its disintegration . . . by adherence to unrealistic principles and a too meager, too belated sharing of power."

Hayes, Carlton J. H., **A Generation of Materialism:** *1871–1900* (New York: Harper, 1941. $7.95; Torchbooks paperback, $3.25). Carlton Hayes was primarily an intellectual historian, the author of pioneering studies of nineteenth-century nationalism. Here he furnishes a general interpretation of the last three decades of the nineteenth century in Europe. He sees them as the "climax of the Enlightenment" with its cults of science and progress, but also as a period of growing faith in warfare as a legitimate instrument of state policy. Although the "generation of materialism" was singularly free of warfare among the Great Powers, it also witnessed a powerful resurgence of economic nationalism and national imperialism. The long peace did not create habits of peace.

A Generation of Materialism is part of *The Rise of Modern Europe* series. You may also wish to read the next volume in the series, recently published, which continues Hayes's story to the outbreak of war in 1914: Oron J. Hale's **The Great Illusion:** *1900–1914* (New York: Harper, 1971. $8.95; Torchbooks paperback, $3.25).

• Hibbert, Christopher, **Garibaldi and His Enemies:** *The Clash of Arms and Personalities in the Making of Italy* (Boston: Little, 1966. $7.50; Plume paperback, $3.95). The warm, romantic figure of Giuseppe Garibaldi is no longer well known outside Italy, but his part in the unification of Italy was crucial. Hibbert has given us a fast-moving sympathetic account of his life that unites accuracy of detail with the fluency of historical fiction. Garibaldi, as Hibbert points out, "was not a clever man. He was more inclined to be ruled by instinct than by reasoning. He saw problems starkly without gradations of emphasis. But this very lack of *chiaroscuro* in his vision, this certainty unclouded by doubt, had always been the main source of his power and of his influence."

Hobsbawm, E. J., **The Age of Revolution:** *1789–1848* (Cleveland: World, 1962. Reprinted by New York: Praeger, $10.00; Mentor paperback, $1.50). Hobsbawm, a young Marxist historian at the University of London, gives us an interpretative study of the "dual revolution" (in industry and politics) of the years from 1789 to 1848, "the greatest transformation in human history since the remote times when men invented agriculture and metallurgy, writing, the city and the state." In the long run, this transformation has created the modern world. In its immediate impact, it produced the triumph of capitalist industry and middle-class liberal society, which occurred first in Britain and France and soon spread to other parts of the globe. The first part of Hobsbawm's book follows the main developments in the dual revolution, the second part sketches the kind of society it fostered. Hobsbawm ranges widely through such topics as agriculture, *parvenu* careerism, the laboring poor, ideology, the arts, and science. His writing is crisp, his insights are fresh, and he avoids the tedious hectoring and sloganeering that too often spoil Marxist historiography.

Hughes, H. Stuart, **Contemporary Europe:** *A History* [1961] (3rd ed., Englewood Cliffs, N.J.: Prentice, 1971. $10.95). Of the many textbooks of twentieth-century European history, this one by the Harvard intellectual historian H. Stuart Hughes clearly leads the pack. It refuses to get bogged down, as do most of the others, in detailed chronicling of the political history of thirty European countries. Instead, it elects the more difficult strategy of trying to identify patterns of development spanning several countries or the continent as a whole. Not that narrative history is entirely abandoned. Where it is most needed, to trace the course of the world wars, the Russian Revolution, or the rise of fascism in Italy and Germany, Hughes supplies it. But most of his book is interpretative history at its best. Of special value are the chapters on "Technology and Society," "The Culture of the 1920's," and "European Civilization in Crisis."

Jackson, Gabriel, **The Spanish Republic and the Civil War, 1931–1939** (Princeton: Princeton U. P., 1965. $15.00; paperback, $3.45). The Spanish Civil War of 1936–39 has attracted novelists, journalists, painters, film-makers, and historians in great numbers. It was a tragedy of epic proportions, costing more than half a million lives. The intervention of Italy, Germany, Russia, and volunteers from other countries converted it into almost a dress rehearsal of the second World War. But above all it was an event in Spanish history, a right-wing revolution against the democratic republic established in Spain in 1931.

In this detailed history of Spain in the 1930's by an American student of both medieval and modern Spanish history, we gain the kind of perspective that any attempt to understand the Spanish Civil War requires. Jackson sees the period of the Republic and the Civil War as "a great burst of energy motivated by primarily idealistic causes," calling to mind similar explosions in the early history of Spain—the medieval reconquest and assimilation of Moorish Andalusia, the Christianization of America, the leadership of the Counter-Reformation, the fierce resistance mounted against Napoleon in 1808. Eager to bring backward Spain into the modern European world, the leaders of the Republic tried to do too much, too fast. But the failure of the Republic and the coming of the Civil War, Jackson contends, were not inevitable, nor do they prove that Spaniards are incapable of political democracy. Another excellent book, livelier in style, although less adequate in scholarship and grasp of Spanish
● history, is Hugh Thomas, **The Spanish Civil War** (New York: Harper, 1961. $12.50; Colophon paperback, $3.45).

Lafore, Laurence, **The Long Fuse:** *An Interpretation of the Origins of World War I* [1965] (2nd ed., Philadelphia: Lippincott, 1971. $4.50; paperback, $2.45). Lafore assigns the greatest share of responsibility for the War of 1914 to the long-standing quarrel between Austria-Hungary and Serbia. He writes a clear and colorful history of the origins of the Austro-Serbian conflict, tracing it back through the events of half a century to its sources in the multi-national composition of the Habsburg monarchy, which rendered it fatally vulnerable to the intrigues of

Serbian nationalism. This was the one problem that was "neither negotiable nor repressible" during the international crisis of the summer of 1914. A whole library of books has been written about the origins of the first World War, but this to my mind is the best. Representative excerpts from the historiographical debate on the war's origins are available in Dwight E. Lee, ed., **The Outbreak of the First World War:** *Who or What Was Responsible?* [1958] (3rd ed., Boston: Heath, 1970. Paperback, $2.25).

Lefebvre, Georges, **The French Revolution** [1930] (2 vols., New York: Columbia U.P., 1962–64. $12.00 and $10.00; paperback, $3.45 each). In France, the history of the French Revolution is a major scholarly industry, with its own journals, societies, and university chairs. Here a former holder of the chair in the history of the Revolution at the Sorbonne sums up his life's work. Lefebvre strongly sympathized with the aims of the more radical leaders of the Revolution. As a socialist, he looked on the Thermidorean reaction of 1794 with candid disapproval. But his treatment of the whole revolutionary decade to 1799 is generally fair-minded, and we can be grateful to the translators for making this important book available in English. A shorter and sometimes livelier study of the same years is Crane Brinton's **A Decade of Revolution:** *1789–1799* (New York: Harper, 1934. $7.95; Torchbooks paperback, $2.45).

Levi, Albert William, **Philosophy and the Modern World** (Bloomington, Ind.: Indiana U.P., 1959. Paperback, $5.45). Levi has written a sophisticated history and critique of the main currents of twentieth-century Western thought. The academic philosophers examined include Bergson, Dewey, Russell, Carnap, Jaspers, Sartre, Moore, Wittgenstein, and Whitehead. There are also chapters on historical thought (Spengler and Toynbee), psychoanalysis (Freud and his followers), political and economic thought (Lenin and Veblen), and the revolution in physics (Einstein and Planck). In addition, Levi provides two stimulating introductory essays on "fragmentation" and the conflict between "rationality and irrationality" as problems in modern thought, viewed in historical perspective. "The intellectual crisis of the modern world," he notes, "is the heritage of the unresolved conflicts of the eighteenth and nineteenth centuries." His book is the best guide available to the intellectual history of twentieth-century Europe.

● Markham, Felix, **Napoleon** (New York: New American, 1964. Paperback, $1.25). There have been relatively few biographies in English of the emperor from Corsica. He was a curious mixture of enlightened reformer, upstart military dictator, and would-be builder of a new Roman empire. Even if he had succeeded in conquering Europe, Markham doubts that his empire "could have lasted more than a few years." But for the history of France, Napoleon's career was decisive. "The legal, administrative and social institutions which he stamped on France, still malleable from the fiery furnace of the Revolution, remain the lasting monument to his genius." This is a compact history of Napoleon and his times, sensible and well written, with a handsome collection of paintings and cartoons of the Napoleonic era.

● For a still briefer account, see Herbert Butterfield, **Napoleon** [1939] (Collier paperback, $0.95). A first-rate history of Napoleonic Europe is Geoffrey Bruun, **Europe and the French Imperium:** *1799–1814* [1938] (2nd ed., New York: Harper, 1957. $7.95; Torchbooks paperback, $2.25).

● Moorehead, Alan, **The Russian Revolution** (New York: Harper, 1958. $7.95. Perennial paperback, $0.95). Based in part on research in the secret archives of the German Foreign Office, this widely read history of the Russian Revolution argues that "the Germans played an important role in bringing Lenin and the Bolsheviks to power." About half of it is devoted to the dramatic events of 1917–18, the rest to the backgrounds of the Revolution in earlier Russian history. Moorehead's prose is charged with vitality, and this is good popular history, but for more scholarly accounts, consult R. V. Daniels, **Red October:** *The Bolshevik Revolution of 1917* (New York: Scribner, 1967. Paperback, $3.45), and the detailed narrative in E. H. Carr, **The Bolshevik Revolution,** *1917–1923* (3 vols., New York: Macmillan, 1950–53. $7.50 each; 3 vols., Penguin paperback, $2.25, $2.45, and $2.45).

Morazé, Charles, **The Triumph of the Middle Classes:** *A Study of European Values in the Nineteenth Century* [1957] (Cleveland: World, 1967. Anchor paperback, $2.95). "The year 1900 was a wonderful one, when men were proud to be middle-class, and to be Europeans. The fate of the whole world was decided around green baize-covered tables in London, Paris or Berlin. . . . So much power had never before been concentrated in so few hands within so small an area of the globe. It was the age of triumph of the European middle classes. This book sets out to explain how this power was built up."

So begins Charles Morazé's social and economic history of nineteenth-century Europe. A few paragraphs later he lets the cat out of the bag. "The middle classes of nineteenth-century Europe conquered the world not because they were middle class or European, but because they were more capable than their predecessors, or than leaders in other parts of the world, of exploiting the technical weapons put into men's hands by the progress of science." Bourgeois Europe's monopoly of science, pure and applied, did not last long. By the end of the nineteenth century, the United States and Russia had already begun to challenge her world leadership. Asia was soon to follow. But while it lasted, the ascendancy of bourgeois Europe was something to behold. The old courtly society founded on privilege disappeared forever, and nothing could be the same again. This is a lucid study of how science, industrial and political revolution, the rise of the middle class, and the new imperialism of nineteenth-century Europe worked together to make the modern world.

Palmer, R. R., **The Age of the Democratic Revolution:** *A Political History of Europe and America, 1760–1800* (2 vols., Princeton: Princeton U.P., 1959–64. $13.50 each; paperback, ● $2.95 each. Abridged and revised as **The World of the French Revolution,** New York: Harper, 1971. $8.50; Torchbooks paperback, $2.95). R. R. Palmer suggests that the revolutions of the last third of the eighteenth century in Europe and America constituted a single trans-Atlantic revolution. It was a "democratic revolution," an assault on the power of aristocracies and the institutions through which aristocracies sought to control the sociopolitical order. The American Revolution was one expression of this larger movement; Palmer sees the struggle in America as much more than a war for national independence. The French Revolution was another expression. But one can also see the democratic revolution at work in the birth of a new radicalism in Britain, and its campaign to reform Parliament; and in anti-establishment political movements that erupted even before 1789 in the Lowlands, Geneva, Italy, and elsewhere. Palmer's first volume, entitled *The Challenge,* studies the period from 1760 to 1792. In the second volume, *The Struggle,* he offers an interpretative synthesis of the international democratic revolution of the 1790's, when radical hopes for a new France came to fulfillment and similar hopes blazed in almost every country in Europe. Democracy suffered many setbacks in the years that followed, but "all revolutions since 1800 . . . have learned from the eighteenth-century Revolution of Western Civilization. They have been inspired by its successes, echoed its ideals, used its methods."

Palmer, R. R., and Joel Colton, **A History of the Modern World** [1950] (4th ed., New York: Knopf, 1971. $11.95). This is one of the most successful college textbooks in publishing history. Its success is well earned. Although it weaves in material on the Americas, Asia, and Africa, and opens with several chapters on the Middle Ages and the early modern centuries, it remains primarily a history of modern Europe, stressing the development of European civilization as a whole. Politics form the core of concern, but there is also generous coverage of social, economic, and cultural history. Best of all, I think, are the book's succinct, provocative generalizations, which never reach the "cosmic" level, but do help the student gain a clearer understanding of the major trends in modern European and world history.

Pinson, Koppel S., **Modern Germany:** *Its History and Civilization* [1954] (2nd ed., New York: Macmillan, 1966. $10.95). Pinson's history of Germany since the French Revolution is an exceptionally fine college textbook. Readers will find it valuable, above all, for its treatment of economic and cultural history. A final chapter covers the Adenauer era. See also Hajo Holborn's **A History of Modern Germany:** *1840–1945* (New York: Knopf, 1969. $10.50).

Robertson, Priscilla, **Revolutions of 1848:** *A Social History* (Princeton: Princeton U.P., 1952. $11.00; paperback, $2.95). "No one," writes Priscilla Robertson, "has ever numbered the revolutions which broke out in Europe in 1848. Counting those in the small German states, the Italian states, and the provinces of the Austrian Empire, there must have been over fifty." She limits her study to just a few. The big one in France earns five chapters, the revolutions in Germany three, with ten more chapters for Vienna, Hungary, Milan, Rome, and Venice. Yet all these revolutions seemed to achieve nothing. They aroused pathological fears of mass violence in the propertied classes and led to fratricidal conflict between the two revolutionary classes: the bourgeoisie and the workers. "Out of 1848 and its struggles no important new freedom was wrested. . . . After 1848 classes and nations played power politics, each unashamed to get what it could each for itself with very little thought for the common welfare of society." The last bitter harvest of the failure of liberal democracy was reaped in the twentieth century, when Europe resorted to total wars and total states in a desperate effort to solve the problems left unsolved in 1848.

Stavrianos, L. S., **The Balkans since 1453** (New York: Holt, 1958. $15.75). As a graduate student, I began my work in the field of Balkan history, and soon deserted it for greener pastures. One reason for my desertion is probably that L. S. Stavrianos had not yet published *The Balkans since 1453*. At the time, no comprehensive survey of Balkan history in English was available, except for a sadly outdated volume by Ferdinand Schevill. The Balkans are a fascinating and beautiful corner of Europe, but they include so many countries and languages so little known to most Americans that we need all the help we can get in understanding them. Stavrianos, in this definitive general history, studies the period of Ottoman Turkish rule, the great age of Balkan revolutionary nationalism (1815–1878), and the history of the Balkan states (Greece, Serbia/Yugoslavia, Albania, Bulgaria, and Rumania) since their winning of independence, to the end of the second World War. He furnishes a huge bibliography, and a well chosen assortment of plates and maps.

Stearns, Peter N., **European Society in Upheaval:** *Social History since 1800* (New York: Macmillan, 1967. $7.95; paperback, $4.95). As the study of history enters the 1970's, it seems clear that the field with the highest growth potential is social history. The scandalous indifference of older scholars to such topics as population, class and family structure, schooling, social mobility, urbanization, the rites of life and death, and the status of women is now being corrected. Peter Stearns is a good example of the new breed of social historians, and *European Society in Upheaval* is a clearly organized and comprehensive outline of modern European social history from the French Revolution to the present day. Throughout, he centers his analysis on the impact of demographic growth and industrialization on both rural and urban society. "The basic fact of European history since 1800 has been an unprecedented social upheaval," an upheaval that has "left its mark on every aspect of modern European history."

Taylor, A. J. P., **The Habsburg Monarchy, 1809–1918:**
A History of the Austrian Empire and Austria-Hungary [1942]
(rev. ed., New York: Macmillan, 1948. Reprinted by New York:
Humanities, $5.50; Torchbooks paperback, $2.45). The one
Great Power in Europe that hardly any American student of
history knows is Austria. There is no market for books about her,
because she has now dwindled to the size of Portugal or Bulgaria,
and plays no role at all in contemporary international power
struggles. But for almost four centuries, Habsburg Austria ruled
central Europe.

In this excellent study by A. J. P. Taylor, one of a small
handful of good books available in English for any period of
Habsburg history, we follow the decline and fall of Austrian
power from the appointment of Prince Metternich as foreign minister in 1809 to the final dissolution of the empire in 1918. Taylor
does not buy the argument of many Austrophiles that the empire had a chance of succeeding. In an age of independent nation-
states, Habsburg Austria was a hopeless anachronism, a bundle
of lands held together only by the imperial crown and the superior
position granted to its German (and after 1867 also its Hungarian) citizens. The subject Slavs, Rumanians, and others were not
to be appeased. "Inevitably, any concession came too late and
was too little; and equally inevitably every concession produced
more violent discontent. The national principle, once launched,
had to work itself out to its conclusion."

● Taylor, A. J. P., **The Origins of the Second World War**
(New York: Atheneum, 1961. $6.95; Premier paperback,
$0.95). The most controversial of Taylor's many books is this
one, in which he challenges the generally accepted doctrine that
Nazi Germany and its Führer bear full responsibility for the war
that broke out in 1939. On the contrary, says Taylor, there is no
hard evidence that Hitler seriously planned a general European
or world war. To be sure, he sought to nullify the hated Treaty

of Versailles and restore Germany to the ranks of the Great
Powers, as any German statesman in an age of unbridled nationalism would naturally want to do, and as many Western ob-
servers agreed he had the right to do. But the war that came in
1939, "far from being premeditated, was a mistake, the result on
both sides of diplomatic blunders." Only in 1941, after success
on the Western front had gone to his head, did Hitler turn this
accidental war into a bid for imperial conquest on a grand scale,
by attacking his former ally Soviet Russia.

Taylor has drawn as many hostile critics as a side of beef
left out in the sun will draw flies, but he may well be right. The
horror of Nazi war-time policies in occupied Europe should not
blind us to the fairly conventional realities of the international
power game played between 1936 and 1940. See also J. W.
Wheeler-Bennett's **Munich:** *Prologue to Tragedy* (New York:
Duell, 1948) and Laurence Lafore, **The End of Glory:** *An Interpretation of the Origins of World War II* (Philadelphia: Lippincott, 1970. $5.95; paperback, $2.45).

●   Tuchman, Barbara W., **The Proud Tower:** *A Portrait of
the World before the War, 1890–1914* (New York: Macmillan,
1966. $7.95; Bantam paperback, $1.45). "The Great War of
1914–18 lies like a band of scorched earth dividing that time
from ours. . . . This book is an attempt to discover the quality of
the world from which the Great War came." Tuchman's interest
centers not on the diplomatic crises beloved by political historians
but on the texture of European and American society in the quar-
ter-century that preceded 1914. It was a proud, vital, explosive
society, happy for the rich, full of frustration for the poor. It was
also a guilty society: "a phenomenon of such extended malig-
nance as the Great War does not come out of a Golden Age."

The Proud Tower is a masterpiece of popular history. It
includes vivid sketches of prewar English political life, the
Anarchist movement, the Dreyfus case, the Hague peace con-

ferences of 1899 and 1907, the career of the German composer
Richard Strauss, and the socialists of the 1890–1914 era. Tuchman closes with a fateful scene: the assassination in a Paris café
of Jean Jaurès. He had worked harder than any other leader of
international socialism to persuade workers not to fight in the
event of a new "capitalist" war. He was shot on July 31, 1914,
and World War One began the next day.

Von Laue, Theodore H., **Why Lenin? Why Stalin?:** *A
Reappraisal of the Russian Revolution, 1900–1930* [1964] (2nd
ed., Philadelphia: Lippincott, 1971. $3.95; paperback, $2.45).
This is a book of special importance to students of world history.
It views 1917 not only as an event in Russian and European history, but as the first in a new category of revolutions, "the revolution of the underdeveloped countries." Von Laue bases his con-
tention on a further point: Russia was not, despite all her efforts
since Peter the Great, a Western country. The peculiar Western
combination of private and local initiative with national political
discipline that made possible the rapid industrial progress of
countries like England and France did not exist in tsarist Russia
and could not exist in the Russia ruled by Lenin and Stalin. State
planning and coercion had to accomplish alone the tasks shared
in the West by the "private sector." Tsarism itself had initiated
this revolution of modernization when Sergei Witte served as
Minister of Finance (1892–1903) under Nicholas II. Lenin and
Stalin finished what Witte had begun, and with the same basic
instrument: the power of the omnipotent state. Marxism played
no part at all after 1917, except as window dressing to help lure
unwary customers into the shop.

The implication for today's world is obvious. "Having
pioneered the techniques of social control for the adopting of
western technology, the Russian Communists can justly proffer
the gist of their experience to other peoples who find themselves

in similar straits. As a model of limited scope, they have not been unsuccessful. Among the countries risen to statehood after the end of World War II, we find hardly one which . . . has not deliberately copied some feature of the Soviet system."

●   Woodham-Smith, C. B., **The Reason Why** [1954] (2nd ed., New York: McGraw, 1971. $7.95; Dutton paperback, $1.95). Woodham-Smith's problem in this modern classic of military and social history is to explain one of the great fiascos of all times: why a brigade of British light cavalry was ordered to attack a position heavily defended by Russian artillery during the Crimean War. "Theirs not to reason why," wrote Tennyson. "Theirs but to do and die." The pointless doing and dying, the author discovers, can be understood only by making a careful study of the personalities of the British commanders involved and the system by which commissions were acquired in the British army. Her analysis is convincing, her story-telling powers are formidable.

    Wright, Gordon, **The Ordeal of Total War:** *1939–1945* (New York: Harper, 1968. $8.95; Torchbooks paperback, $2.75). The twentieth and last volume in *The Rise of Modern Europe* series, Wright's history of the second World War combines economy of means with breadth of view. In just over 300 pages, he narrates the military and political history of the war, analyzes the economics of total war, discusses the contributions of propaganda and science, surveys German rule and underground resistance in occupied Europe, and sums up the impact of the war on politics, society, thought, and culture. Not to mention a 35-page bibliographical essay! He offers no startling or bold new interpretations of the war, but he leaves his readers with no doubts that its "destructive impact on the continent of Europe probably exceeds that of any previous disaster in the modern era." At the same time, early postwar fears that the war marked "the end of the European age" have turned out to be premature. "A quarter-century after the conflict, one can no longer be sure that Europe as a major locus of power and of high culture is extinct; the Jeremiahs of 1945 had failed to take account of the recuperative powers of an old continent."

chapter	The World
nine	Since
	1945

Anyone standing in the ruins of Berlin or Leningrad or Hiroshima in the autumn of 1945 might have been tempted to wax melancholy about the fate of the modern world. Despite all the growing, all the democratizing, all the industrializing, European civilization and its zealous imitators in the other continents had managed to blow themselves up in an orgy of killing that still defies statistical analysis. In the future one could reasonably expect another calamitous postwar depression, another round of fascist tyrants, and, finally, nuclear Armageddon.

Instead, western Europe recovered, the most devastated countries just as swiftly as the least devastated. Soviet Russia, which suffered the worst losses during Hitler's war, also returned to buoyant health. The persecuted Jews staggered to their feet and some of them built the long-dreamed Zionist national state in Palestine. The United States, where the Great Crash of 1929 had started, went from peak to peak under administrations of both parties. Japan, whose industry was almost wiped out, became an economic superpower and surpassed all but a few Western countries. An enfeebled, feudal, warlord-ridden China changed almost overnight into a feared and respected "people's democracy." The colonial populations of Asia and Africa threw off their white masters in wars and movements of national liberation that rival in heroism the struggles for independence of old America or old Europe. Fascism has not revived. The third World War has not happened.

So far, so good. But of course the history of the world since 1945 has not been all roses. The other side of the picture is the Cold War and the unchecked nuclear arms race; the widening gap between the industrially advanced and the industrially retarded countries; the first signs of an ecological crisis that may nullify all the gains of technology; a continuing uneasiness of spirit among all segments of the world's peoples; and social, economic, political, and cultural change still happening too fast for institutions or ideas to keep pace with it. Any fair-minded person looking at the world since 1945 in the context of the early 1970's can say only one thing: it is still too early to be sure. We have won a temporary reprieve from disaster, but as any Greek tragedian could tell you, things always look best just before the fall.

In this last chapter, the problem of finding suitable books becomes a little more difficult again. The number of indubitable classics shrinks. This is unavoidable. But I strongly believe that the study of world history cannot stop at this or that mysteriously chosen date. World history never stops, and the world historian (bless his tired feet!) cannot afford to stop running. We must even spare a little time in our studies and in our courses for an earnest consideration of the "foreseeable" future—which, in due course, will be just as dead and gone as the past we try to call to life today.

Barraclough, Geoffrey, **An Introduction to Contemporary History** (New York: Basic, 1965. Penguin paperback, $1.45). Barraclough contends that Europe's once dominant role in world affairs has ended. He winds up the "modern" or "European" era in the early 1960's, but the beginning of the end came in the 1890's, when the new scientific industrialism of the late nineteenth century had transformed European society and Europe had reached out to gather the rest of the planet under her wing. Since she could not retain monopolistic control of her science and technology, the powers she set free at the close of the nineteenth century were inevitably acquired by America, Africa, and Asia. In place of the modern age came the "contemporary" or "postmodern" age of decolonization, mass democracy, and a new art and literature of social commitment. "Between the Suez crisis of 1882 and the Suez crisis of 1956, the wheel turned full circle; and in the interval the transition from one period of history to another took place." Middle-class Europe, with her dreary self-enchanted aesthetes, prancing fascist fuhrers, and lofty colonial administrators, had ceased to matter. "The European age . . . is over, and with it the predominance of the old European scales of values."

Boulding, Kenneth E., **The Meaning of the Twentieth Century:** *The Great Transition* (New York: Harper, 1964. $5.00; Colophon paperback, $1.95). This short book supplies an incisive analysis of present tendencies in world civilization and a series of warnings and prescriptions for the future. Boulding regards the twentieth century as "the middle period of a great transition in the state of the human race." Just as humankind made the transition from barbarism to civilization some five thousand years ago, so now it is making the transition, powered by modern science, to "postcivilized society," a world of automation, planet-wide loyalties, and the rule (Boulding hopes) of peace and reason.

Brown, W. Norman, **The United States and India, Pakistan, Bangladesh** [1953] (rev. ed., Cambridge, Mass.: Harvard U.P., 1972. $15.00; paperback, $3.95). Except for a chapter on

U.S. relations with the subcontinent, this is a study of modern India and Pakistan: their traditional heritage, the effects of British rule, the movement for independence, and their postwar history. Three-quarters of the book deals with the postwar period. Inevitably, much of Brown's narrative centers on the partition of British India into two hostile states, with its tragic accompaniment of race riots and mass migrations of peoples on a scale that stuns the mind. The partition "struck the subcontinent where it lived. It disrupted its economy, its communications, its administration. It weakened its defense. It divided it into mutually antipathetic and suspicious nations, with a clashing cultural discord inherited from a long past. . . . It was, in fact, a subcontinental disaster." Brown also examines the domestic politics of India and Pakistan, their social problems, economic life, and foreign affairs. The current edition includes an account of the emergence of the newly independent state of Bangladesh, formerly East Pakistan.

Brzezinski, Zbigniew K., **The Soviet Bloc:** *Unity and Conflict* [1960] (rev. ed., Cambridge, Mass.: Harvard U.P., 1967. $15.00; paperback, $3.75). Brzezinski's aim in this book is to study the relations among the states of the Communist "camp" since the second World War. His special interest is the interaction of Communist ideology and the political institutions of the Communist countries. The Sino-Soviet conflict, he writes, has been for international Communism "a tragic disaster, comparable in some respects to the split in Christianity several centuries ago." Peking now rivals Moscow, and most of Russia's former satellite states have become "junior allies." Soviet power remains, but only as one actor among several in an increasingly complex international system.

Crankshaw, Edward, **Khrushchev:** *A Career* (New York: Viking, 1966. $7.50; Compass paperback, $2.75). N. S. Khrushchev for nearly a decade filled the power vacuum left by the death of Joseph Stalin. Under his rule, Russia was "de-Stalinized," the Hungarian revolution was suppressed, new alliances were forged in the Caribbean and the Middle East, China left the Soviet bloc, Soviet provocations in Berlin and Cuba threatened to ignite World War Three, better relations were established with the United States, Soviet control of eastern Europe was relaxed, and Russia amazed the world by gaining a long lead in the "space race."

The British journalist Edward Crankshaw's biography of the man at the top was not, one suspects, the most difficult book in the world to write. Very much unlike Stalin, Khrushchev made no mystery of himself. Unsophisticated, colorful, outspoken, by turns ruthless and humane, he lingers in memory like a Russian Harry Truman. Crankshaw gives him only limited credit for the better features of his regime. Although he became, at the end, something of a real statesman, Khrushchev remained the prisoner of his own past. "He moved backwards into the future, trying to stand at bay, but always giving ground to the forces he himself, to his own greater glory, had unloosed."

● Eichelberger, Clark M., **UN:** *The First Twenty-Five Years* [1965] (4th ed., New York: Harper, 1970. $5.95). The author of this short book on the work of the United Nations is one of the U.N.'s staunchest defenders. He does not mince his words: during the last quarter-century, "the decisive factor for world peace has been the United Nations. It has made the difference between the uneasy peace in which the world has lived and a third world war." Even the Cuba missile crisis, Eichelberger feels, would have ended in war without the intervention of the Security Council and the good offices of Secretary-General U Thant. His book reviews the peace-keeping role of the U.N.; studies its record in disarmament, human rights, and economic and social assistance; and recommends ways of making it significantly stronger in future years.

Emerson, Rupert, **From Empire to Nation:** *The Rise to Self-Assertion of Asian and African Peoples* (Cambridge, Mass.: Harvard U.P., 1960. $12.00; Beacon paperback, $2.95). This is not so much a history of the collapse of European imperialism as an analysis of the pattern of nation-building in postwar Asia and Africa. The key development in Emerson's view has been the rise of a European-type nationalism. The West has lost its colonies but it "has scored an extraordinary triumph in that it is more than ever the model to which other countries look in their drive for development." Summarizing the Afro-Asian response to the West, Emerson discerns three phases: an initial xenophobic reaction against everything Western, illustrated by the Boxer Rebellion and the Mahdist revolt in the Sudan; a period of self-humiliating acceptance of Western superiority; and the "nationalist synthesis" of recent decades, when Asians and Africans have recovered pride in their heritage, but at the same time seek to follow the Western example by developing modern industrialized nation-states. On the whole, nationalism has been a constructive force, but Emerson hopes that the new nations will not "follow the ruinous course of their cantankerous predecessors upon the national stage" by engaging in vicious fratricidal wars.

Falk, Richard A., **This Endangered Planet:** *Prospects and Proposals for Human Survival* (New York: Random, 1971. $8.95; Vintage paperback, $2.95). Richard A. Falk is a professor of international law at Princeton, and a major figure in contemporary thinking about world legal and political order. In this vitally important book, he reaches beyond the problems of international law to assess the crisis in our civilization as a whole: the threats posed by "the war system," but also the towering dangers of world overpopulation, the depletion of natural resources, and the general deterioration of the environmental life-support systems of "spaceship earth." He sketches designs for a new world order that could bring these dangers under control without necessarily creating a world government in the classic sense of the term. More radical prescriptions may be studied in two books of my own: W. Warren Wagar, **The City of Man:** *Prophecies of a World Civilization in Twentieth-Century Thought* (Boston: Houghton, 1963. Penguin paperback, $1.65), and **Building the City of Man:** *Outlines of a World Civilization* (New York: Grossman, 1971. $10.00; Freeman paperback, $3.25).

FitzGerald, Frances, **Fire in the Lake:** *The Vietnamese and the Americans in Vietnam* (Boston: Little, 1972. $12.50). "Fire in the Lake" is the classical Chinese image of revolution, from the *I Ching* or "Book of Changes." Throughout this illuminating study of the Vietnam war and its place in Vietnamese history, the author stresses the roots of the conflict in the political and intellectual traditions of the Vietnamese people. She finds that even the Communists, both in the North and in the South, fit the ancient mould closely.

The first half of her book reviews the history of Vietnam and the outbreak of the revolution in South Vietnam during the Diem regime. In the second half, she follows the Americanization of the war from the Kennedy years to the spring of 1971. The massive U.S. presence in South Vietnam, she believes, made eventual national unification under revolutionary leadership all the more certain. The Americans "destroyed the economic base" of the South, as well as the regional political groups that held out against unification. "They have . . . flattened the local ethnic, religious, and cultural peculiarities beneath a uniform, national disaster." Soon the time will arrive "for the narrow flame of revolution to cleanse the lake of Vietnamese society from the corruption and disorder of the American war." Good accounts of the earlier war against the French are available in Ellen J. Hammer,**The Struggle for Indochina, 1940-1955:** *Vietnam and the French Experience* [1954] (rev. ed., Stanford: Stanford U.P., 1966. $10.00; paperback, $2.95), and Bernard B. Fall, **The Two**

Viet-Nams: *A Political and Military Analysis* [1963] (3rd ed., New York: Praeger, 1967. $10.00).

Hatch, John, **A History of Postwar Africa** (New York: Praeger, 1965. $10.00; paperback, $3.95). "The African political revolution has been the most dramatic international phenomenon since the war. Within a few years more than thirty new nations were born." Several others have come into existence since this book was written, but it remains a convenient survey of the politics of liberation in postwar Africa. Hatch sees the African independence movements as primarily "anti-colonial," not "nationalist." Nationalities in the European sense were not a feature of the African political landscape, but African politicians chose to accept the boundaries drawn by the colonial powers "rather than confuse their movements by trying to define new national units." The way was led by Ghana, which achieved independence in 1957. "It was Kwame Nkrumah and his colleagues," Hatch notes, "who had both set the compass and forced the pace." For the problems faced by the new African countries since the winning of independence, two excellent books are Basil Davidson,
● **Which Way Africa?:** *The Search for a New Society* [1964] (3rd ed., Baltimore: Penguin, 1971. Paperback, $1.95), and Ruth First, **Power in Africa** (New York: Pantheon, 1970. $10.00; Penguin paperback, $2.95).

Hopkins, Harry, **Egypt, the Crucible:** *The Unfinished Revolution in the Arab World* (Boston: Houghton, 1970. $10.00). Most Westerners are infected, as Harry Hopkins points out, by a new anti-Semitism aimed not at Jews but at Arabs, and above all at the people of Egypt. Admiration for Israel and fears for her safety in the face of Arab threats of extermination make it almost impossible for the typical Westerner, Jewish or Gentile, to understand the Egyptian point of view in the Arab-Israeli confrontation or to look with any real sympathy on the achievements of Arab socialism in Egypt since the revolution that sent King Farouk packing in 1952.

In a vivid account of Egyptian history in the postrevolutionary generation, Hopkins gives his readers a chance to see "the other side" of the argument, to rectify "the more persistent distortions of the lens through which we have lately been in the habit of seeing the Arab world." Most of his book is devoted to studies of the political, social, economic, and cultural modernization of Egypt under Nasser, which he compares favorably to the progress made by Israel during the same period. There are also several chapters on Egyptian-Israeli relations. Throughout, Hopkins tends to agree, although not slavishly, with the policies of the Nasser regime. He favors the establishment of a multinational state in the eastern Mediterranean, a new Levantine state purged of "narrow nationalism" and Zionist *apartheid,* in which Jews, Christians, and Muslims can work together toward common goals.

Hurewitz, J. C., **Middle East Politics:** *The Military Dimension* (New York: Praeger, 1969. $11.50; paperback, $4.95). During the Middle Ages, in both Christendom and Islam, states were created by warriors. Only in the nineteenth and early twentieth centuries did the models of the "bourgeois" and "proletarian" state emerge, polities made and run by civilians, although they sometimes had to stage a violent revolution to win power. Even Lenin, Stalin, Mussolini, and Hitler were civilians. In the post-1945 world, there has been—perhaps ominously—a trend toward military states once again, not only in Latin America, where they were common in the nineteenth century, but in Africa and Asia as well.

In this comprehensive survey, J. C. Hurewitz looks at the phenomenon of military politics in the Middle East since World War Two. He explores its roots in the Islamic and European traditions, studies the impact of the Cold War, discusses armies as agencies of social change in the Middle East, and furnishes a country-by-country review of political-military interaction in eighteen Middle Eastern states. Only three of these are found to be "non-military republics" (Israel, Lebanon, and Tunisia), and one of the three (Israel) is aptly labeled a "garrison democracy." This is a brilliant and sophisticated book, in which the author skillfully integrates political, military, social, economic, and even intellectual history.

•   Lukacs, John, **A New History of the Cold War** [1961] (3rd ed., Garden City, N.Y.: Doubleday, 1966. Anchor paperback, $2.50). The Cold War, writes Lukacs, began in 1945–47 when Germany and most of Europe were divided into American and Soviet spheres of influence. Stalin seized the opportunity to create an empire of satellite states in his sphere, moved not by considerations of Marxist ideology but by an expansive Russian nationalism that the United States at first naively tolerated and then hastily sought to counter. The struggle reached a turning point in 1956, when the United States refused to risk general war to save Hungary. In 1962 Soviet Russia showed a similar disinclination to fight for her missile bases in Cuba. Since then the Cold War has undergone "decrystallization," thanks to the nuclear balance of terror, the rift between Russia and China, and the gradual corrosion of the Iron Curtain as the eastern European people's democracies liberalize their regimes and restore trade links with the West.

     A Hungarian who emigrated to the United States in 1946, Lukacs makes little attempt to conceal his anti-Communist, anti-Russian bias. The Western position is also forcefully stated by David Rees in **The Age of Containment:** *The Cold War, 1945–1965* (New York: St. Martin's, 1967. $5.95; paperback, $2.25). The Soviet view receives a more favorable reading in D. F. Fleming, **The Cold War and Its Origins, 1917–1960** (2 vols., Garden City, N.Y.: Doubleday, 1961. $17.95 the set).

     Myrdal, Gunnar, **Asian Drama:** *An Inquiry into the Poverty of Nations* (3 vols., New York: Twentieth Century, 1968. 3 vols., Pantheon paperback, $10.00 the set. Abridged as

An Approach to the Asian Drama, Methodological and Theoretical, New York: Random, 1970. Vintage paperback, $3.95. Shorter abridgement by Seth King under original title, New York: Pantheon, 1972. $10.00; Vintage paperback, $1.95). This is the sort of book that will use up every rainy day of your vacation, and perhaps a few of the sunny ones, too. Abridgements are available, but the complete work with its three volumes and 2,284 pages, written by the eminent Swedish economist Gunnar Myrdal in collaboration with a large staff of research workers and consultants, is the most ambitious public report ever filed on what some people would call the number one problem of the postwar era: the steadily widening gap between the rich and poor nations of the world.

In spite of its length, *Asian Drama* does not cover all the "underdeveloped" countries. Myrdal limited his attention to South Asia—India, Pakistan, Ceylon, Burma, Malaya, Thailand, Indonesia, and the Philippines. Within this area, the Indian experience is studied with special thoroughness. Political problems and economic realities are the topics of the first volume; the second investigates economic planning, labor, and population; health, education, and welfare are surveyed in the third.

Myrdal suggests that solutions for Asia's poverty will not be found unless all concerned realize that "the basic social and economic structure of the countries of South Asia is radically different from that existing in advanced Western countries." He attacks the short-sighted and ignorant aid policies of the West and the failure of leadership in the underdeveloped countries themselves. His proposals for change are summed up in a more recent book, **The Challenge of World Poverty:** *A World Anti-Poverty Program in Outline* (New York: Pantheon, 1970. $8.95; Vintage paperback, $2.95), which also reviews the main points made in *Asian Drama*.

●   Myrdal, Jan, and Gun Kessle, **Chinese Journey** (New

York: Pantheon, 1965. $9.95; Beacon paperback, $2.95). In 1962 two Swedes—the writer Jan Myrdal and his artist-wife Gun Kessle—were given permission to spend a year living in a small village in northwestern China. During this time, they also traveled in Inner Mongolia and on the Burma Road. *Chinese Journey* is an impressionistic report of what they saw, with photographs by Kessle and notes by Myrdal. "The pictures," Myrdal admits, "are the most important part of the whole; my text is based on the diary I kept during these journeys. This is no 'objective' description. It is personal. But not private."

•   Paton, Alan, **The Land and People of South Africa** [1955] (rev. ed., Philadelphia: Lippincott, 1972. $3.95). South Africa's best known writer, the author of *Cry, the Beloved Country,* introduces the Republic and its people. Although billed as a juvenile, this is a book that has much to offer readers of any age. Concise, accurate, and fair-minded, but with many personal observations scattered along the way, it is perhaps the best short guide to life in the Republic of South Africa now available.

     Ruiz, Ramon E., **Cuba:** *The Making of a Revolution* (Amherst, Mass.: U. of Mass. Press, 1968. $6.00; Norton paperback, $1.65). Many Americans see Cuba today as little more than a bridgehead of world Communism in the Western hemisphere. But the Revolution of 1959 was an event in Cuban, as well as Communist, history. Ramon Ruiz has written a straightforward study of the political, economic, and ideological background of Castro's rise to power, from the nineteenth century onward. The Cuban revolution, he points out, "represented no sharp break with the past." Even the tactics of guerrilla warfare adopted by Castro's forces in 1956 "followed a blueprint that dated back to the nineteenth century." Ruiz also stresses the importance of anti-Americanism in the Cuban political tradition. Cuba's long dependence on the United States "had a deleterious effect on the Cuban mind. It engendered frustration and rage, especially among the young, over the island's inability to travel alone on the road to nationhood." The texture of Cuban life since 1959 is studied in Rolando E. Bonachea and Nelson P. Valdés, eds., **Cuba in Revolution** (Garden City, N.Y.: Doubleday, 1972. Anchor paperback, $2.95).

Safran, Nadav, **The United States and Israel** (Cambridge, Mass.: Harvard U. P., 1963. $8.50). Like most other volumes in Harvard's excellent but mistitled series *The American Foreign Policy Library,* Safran's has little to say about the United States. Only two chapters deal specifically with U.S.-Israeli relations—and in view of Israel's close ties with America, these are chapters that might appear in any general book on Israel. Safran begins with a discussion of the historic Jewish claim to Palestine, the dynamics of modern Zionism, and the political origins of Israel from the Balfour Declaration to 1947. In the chapters that follow, he examines the country and its people, the pattern of politics, economic life, national defense, and foreign policy. He has also written **From War to War:** *The Arab-Israeli Confrontation, 1948–1967* (New York: Pegasus, 1969. $10.00; paperback, $2.95), a comprehensive history of the Arab-Israeli crisis that includes a full account of the Six Days' War of 1967.

Sampson, Anthony, **The Anatomy of Europe:** *A Guide to the Workings, Institutions and Character of Contemporary Western Europe* (New York: Harper, 1969. $7.95; Colophon paperback, $2.45). What are *au pair* girls? How does the Common Market really work? What is European television like? Why are the left-wing parties in trouble? Who are Europe's campus radicals and what do they want? In which European countries is the most English spoken? These are a few of the many questions you will find answered in Anthony Sampson's survey of western Europe in the 1960's. Although it is full of interesting bits of miscellaneous information, the book also has a more serious purpose: to measure the extent of western Europe's progress toward integration in the postwar era. The search for unity is also the underlying theme of a strikingly illustrated, much shorter volume, **The European Renaissance since 1945** (New York: Harcourt, 1970. $6.95; paperback, $2.95), by the French educator and historian Maurice Crouzet.

Schram, Stuart R., **Mao Tse-tung** (New York: Simon, 1967. $7.95; Penguin paperback, $1.65). Schram's biography of Mao is far from definitive. A career like Mao's, which spans more than half a century, and occupies a place in Chinese history comparable to the place in Russian history of Lenin and Stalin combined, cannot be digested in a book of 350 pages. But Schram is a serious scholar, and his interpretation of Mao's thought and character rings true. He concentrates, wisely enough, on Mao's years as a revolutionary leader, leaving only three chapters for the period since 1949.

The man who takes shape in his narrative and analysis is a tough, intransigent, willful warrior, an exponent of "military romanticism," an extreme nationalist whose "primary concern remains, as it has always been, the fate of China." In sharp contrast to the Russian revolution, which was led from the first by the Bolshevik party created by Lenin, the Maoist revolution has been dominated by the Chinese Red Army. Mao himself has always displayed a "guerrilla mentality," never forgetting that he came to power by building an army from the flesh and blood of the Chinese masses, and by using it skillfully in wars against both Chiang Kai-shek and the Japanese that lasted nearly twenty years. War for Mao Tse-tung is "the supreme adventure and the supreme test of human courage and human will." For a biography more sympathetic to Mao, by a gifted Chinese writer, see Han Suyin, **The Morning Deluge:** *Mao Tse-tung and the Chinese Revolution, 1893–1954* (Boston: Little, 1972. $12.95).

Seton-Watson, Hugh, **The East European Revolution**

[1951] (3rd ed., New York: Praeger, 1956. $6.50; paperback, $3.95). From the American and western European point of view, the one indisputable and unforgivable crime committed by Stalinist Russia after 1945 was its forcible conversion of Poland, Czechoslovakia, and several other eastern European countries into Bolshevized satellite states. Hugh Seton-Watson's book, written during the coldest years of the Cold War, is still a useful summary of the revolutionary changes imposed on the countries of eastern Europe between the end of World War Two and the death of Stalin. It opens with a study of the social and political structure of eastern Europe before 1939 and a detailed account of its participation in the war. Seton-Watson then turns to the period after 1945: the seizure of power by Communist regimes in Poland, Czechoslovakia, Hungary, Rumania, Bulgaria, Yugoslavia, and Albania; economic recovery and state planning; social and religious policy; and the machinery of government.

•   Snow, Edgar, **The Other Side of the River:** *Red China Today* (New York: Random, 1962. Revised as **Red China Today,** New York: Random, 1970. $20.00; Vintage paperback, $3.45). Edgar Snow is famous as the American correspondent who was the first Westerner to interview Mao Tse-tung during the civil war of the 1930's between Mao's Communists and the
• Nationalist government of Chiang Kai-shek. His *Red Star over China* [1937] (rev. ed., New York: Grove, 1968. $10.00; Black Cat paperback, $2.45) is an important document in the early history of Chinese Communism. In *The Other Side of the River,* he gives his impressions of five months of travels in Maoist China in the summer and autumn of 1960. He visited fourteen of China's twenty-two provinces, interviewed more than seventy leaders including Mao and Chou En-lai, and returned with enough material for a shelf of books.

As may be expected, he liked most of what he saw in the new China. He does not doubt that Mao is a dictator, but he reminds us that the Maoist regime did not rob the Chinese people of any freedom they already possessed. The present government "is not a new evil but an old one in a different and lesser or greater degree." It has clearly used its power for more enlightened aims, and with better results, than the corrupt tyranny it overthrew. In addition to reports of his interviews with Mao and Chou, Snow takes us through factories, communes, schools, apartment buildings; discusses the party leadership, minorities policies, cultural life; and much more. This is a sympathetic, entertaining, encyclopedic, but unsubtle portrait of contemporary China.

Szulc, Tad, **The Winds of Revolution:** *Latin America Today—and Tomorrow* [1963] (rev. ed., New York: Praeger, 1965). An irreversible social revolution is taking place in postwar Latin America, writes Tad Szulc, and democracy's urgent challenge "is to demonstrate that a free society can solve its basic social, human, and economic problems as well as or better than a Communist police state." This is a respected journalist's report on Latin America in the 1950's and early 1960's—democracy and dictatorship, population growth, the survival of mass poverty and colonial feudalism, the Cuban Revolution, and the Alliance for Progress. Although recognizing the need for rapid socioeconomic change, Szulc agrees with the architects of John F. Kennedy's Latin American policy that such change must come about "democratically." He applauds U.S. efforts to contain Castroism and stimulate economic growth through collaboration with liberal, reform-minded, middle-class governments such as that of former President Eduardo Frei in Chile.

• Werth, Alexander, **De Gaulle:** *A Political Biography* (New York: Simon, 1966. $7.50; Penguin paperback, $1.65). In a book on modern France published in 1956, Alexander Werth described Charles de Gaulle as "a noble anachronism." In this biography, written while the General was serving as the first president of the Fifth Republic, he gladly eats his words. De Gaulle might like to "impersonate the heir of the old Kings of France," but he also "wants to be the ruler of a thoroughly modern and efficient State" and he had above all "moved with the times." Werth especially admires de Gaulle's foreign policies: his disengagement from Algeria, his advocacy of decolonization and rapprochement with Russia and China, his denunciation of American imperialism in Indochina. Most of the book is concerned with de Gaulle's return to power after 1958, but there are also several chapters on the earlier phases of his career. Werth is not an academic scholar, and least of all a "psychohistorian," but he writes political journalism of the highest caliber.

seventy-five basic books
in world history

There are thousands of "basic books" in a field as big as world history, but the list that follows would make a good personal library for the beginning teacher or graduate student. Junior high school and high school librarians may also find this list useful in book ordering. I have selected some of the best titles from those reviewed above, stressing books with unusual value as reference works. The numbers in parentheses indicate the page on which the book is discussed.

Ashton, T. S., *The Industrial Revolution: 1760–1830* (134)

Bainton, Roland H., *The Reformation of the Sixteenth Century* (96)

Barraclough, Geoffrey, *An Introduction to Contemporary History* (156)

Basham, A. L., *The Wonder That Was India* (75)

Berlin, Sir Isaiah, *Karl Marx* (136)

Billington, James H., *The Icon and the Axe* (90)

Bloch, Marc, *Feudal Society* (91)

Bovill, E. W., *The Golden Trade of the Moors* (124)

Brinton, Crane, *The Anatomy of Revolution* (12, 136)

Bullock, Alan, *Hitler* (136)

Burckhardt, Jacob, *The Civilization of the Renaissance in Italy* (97)

Cantor, Norman F., *Medieval History* (91)

Childe, V. Gordon, *Man Makes Himself* (52)

Creel, H. G., *Confucius The Man and the Myth* (67)

Davidson, Basil, *The African Genius* (126)
Davidson, Basil, *Africa in History* (125)
Deutscher, Isaac, *Stalin* (138)
Dorn, Walter L., *Competition for Empire: 1740–1763* (104)
Elliott, J. H., *Imperial Spain: 1469–1716* (99)
Emerson, Rupert, *From Empire to Nation* (160)
Falls, Cyril, *The Great War: 1914–1918* (139)
Fisher, Sydney N., *The Middle East* (80)
FitzGerald, Frances, *Fire in the Lake* (161)
Friedrich, Carl J., *The Age of the Baroque: 1610–1660* (105)
Garraty, John A., and Peter Gay, eds., *The Columbia History of the World* (40)
Gay, Peter, *The Enlightenment* (106)
Gibbon, Edward, *The Decline and Fall of the Roman Empire* (59)
Gibson, Charles, *Spain in America* (115)
Goodrich, L. Carrington, *A Short History of the Chinese People* (69)
Grattan, C. Hartley, *The Southwest Pacific* (130)
Hall, D. G. E., *A History of South-East Asia* (76)
Herring, Hubert, *A History of Latin America* (115)
Hobsbawn, E. J., *The Age of Revolution: 1789–1848* (141)
Hughes, H. Stuart, *Contemporary Europe* (142)
July, Robert W., *A History of the African People* (128)
Kitto, H. D. F., *The Greeks* (60)
Koestler, Arthur, *The Sleepwalkers* (108)
Langer, William L., ed., *An Encyclopedia of World History* (39)
Lefebvre, Georges, *The French Revolution* (144)
Lewis, Bernard, *The Arabs in History* (83)
Lukacs, John, *A New History of the Cold War* (164)
McNaught, Kenneth, *The History of Canada* (116)
McNeill, William H., *The Rise of the West* (15)
McNeill, William H., *A World History* (16)
Mattingly, Garrett, *The Armada* (100)
Morazé, Charles, *The Triumph of the Middle Classes* (146)
Nehru, Jawaharlal, *The Discovery of India* (78)
Palmer, R. R., *The Age of the Democratic Revolution* (147)

author index